Adopting Enterprise Risk Management

in Today's World:

An Evidence-Based Guide for

Implementation

Adopting Enterprise Risk Management

in Today's World:

An Evidence-Based Guide for

Implementation

by

Dr. Steven Deck

Dedication

This book is dedicated to the people who tirelessly work to reduce risks organizations face in today's fast-paced world. Their efforts sometimes go unnoticed since, if successful, risk managers prevent adverse events from occurring or significantly reduce their impact on the organization. A good day for a risk manager is one that is uneventful with operations continuing without interruption. However, their work is critical to an organization's ability to achieve its mission. By reducing risks that threaten an organization's survival, risk managers preserve the organization's ability to offer people opportunities to earn a living and provide for their families. Indeed, a risk manager role is critical to the success of society even if their work sometimes goes unnoticed.

Acknowledgments

First, I would like to thank my advisory committee for my dissertation, Dr. Thomas Mierzwa and Dr. Denise Breckon. The research for my dissertation served as the foundation for the writing of this book. Their hard work and commitment to my growth as a scholar enabled me to grow intellectually and develop the skills needed to write this book. I would also like to acknowledge Dr. Roger Ward, Senior Vice President for Operations and Institutional Effectiveness and Vice Dean for the Graduate School at the University of Maryland Baltimore for encouraging me to pursue my doctoral degree and continuing to support me throughout my career. Thanks also goes to Dr. Lauren Sweetman for her guidance and editing of this book. Last, and most importantly, I would like to thank my wife, Bonnie, for her patience and support as I fulfilled the demanding requirements of a doctoral program and writing this book.

Biography

Dr. Steven Deck has over 25 years of experience developing and implementing risk management, environmental health and safety, international safety and security, emergency response, and continuity of operation programs and processes in higher education and in biomedical and pharmaceutical industries. Dr. Deck has also lead efforts to identify and treat risks associated with implementing a strategic plan at a large research university. Hence, he has experience managing risks at both the operational and strategic level. He holds a doctorate in management, an MBA, and a bachelor's degree in safety and industrial hygiene management. Dr. Deck also holds an associate in risk management and is a certified industrial hygienist, safety professional, and hazardous materials manager.

Table of Contents

Introduction

Risk is pervasive to conducting business. Consider any operation an organization performs: each requires identifying and managing the risks that can impede the execution of the operation. For example, production units must manage risks such as employee safety or the loss of a critical supplier or piece of equipment, human resource departments confront potential claims of unfair labor practices, and information technology groups must be alert to cyber threats. Moreover, organizations face external risks that arise due to advances in technology, changing economic and market conditions, and increased globalization. Even organizations that fall outside of the traditional conversation on risk must now consider these challenges. Higher education institutions (HEIs), for example, are under increased pressure from the government, public, and campus community to manage risks (The Advisory Board, 2008; University Risk Management and Insurance Association [URMIA], 2007). Such institutions must manage a wide range of risks in diverse areas such as safety and security, regulatory compliance, academic affairs, research, information technology, finance, human resources, and facilities management (Abraham, 2013). Furthermore, recent events such as hurricanes Katrina, Harvey, and

Maria, the economic downturn, and social issues such as sexual assault on campus and protest actions point out the importance of managing risk in higher education. Indeed, although the institution may survive such events, leadership may not. For example, both the Penn State Jerry Sandusky sexual abuse scandal in 2011 and the University of Missouri social protests of 2015 resulted in leadership changes at these institutions.

Many organizations have historically deferred responsibility to managing risks to individual operating units within the organization. However, this approach lacks an overarching strategy for managing risks from an institutional perspective. The lack of a comprehensive risk management strategy leads to inconsistent risk tolerance levels, inefficient resource allocation for risk control activities, and a lack of knowledge on how risk affects achieving the strategic objectives of the organization. Here, an approach known as *enterprise risk management* (ERM) provides a method to manage risks in organizations holistically. In this book, I unpack this approach both theoretically and practically, providing a hands-on guide to understanding, adopting, and implementing ERM within complex organizations. First, however, in the remainder of this introduction, I describe the concept of ERM along with the evidence on which this book is based—

my doctoral research—and the systematic review methodology I employed to analyze it, followed by a brief summary of the structure of the book.

What is ERM?

Enterprise risk management is a senior leadership initiative that aims to integrate an organization's risk management practices in order to enhance the organization's ability to achieve its strategic objectives (The Committee of Sponsoring Organizations [COSO], 2004; Hoyt & Liebenberg, 2011). In doing so, ERM moves beyond traditional risk management approaches that focus on managing risks in functional silos. Instead, ERM aspires to manage risks as a portfolio in order to capture the full range of risks and multiple interdependencies between them. It does this by positioning risk management as a senior leadership responsibility, assessing risk from an entity-wide perspective, aligning business strategies with risk tolerance levels, and integrating accountability for managing risks across the entity (COSO, 2004; Kimbrough & Componation, 2009; Kleffner, Lee, & McGannon, 2003; McShane, Nair, & Rustambekov, 2011). Because of this holistic approach, ERM provides a means to manage organizational risk in a comprehensive and strategic manner.

Existing ERM models originate from the business sector and were developed by practitioners in such fields as auditing, accounting, and insurance (Andersen, 2010). Despite their comprehensive approach, these original frameworks tend to emphasize hierarchal management structures, quantifying risk exposure, and control systems for managing risks. And, as ERM is a relatively new management practice, there is limited empirical research on implementing the practice in complex organizational settings. Therefore, today's organizations face the challenge of introducing useful ERM frameworks that are undeveloped for complex settings into an organizational culture that may already be skeptical of new management approaches due to their previous experiences with restructuring and efforts at organizational change. With the right tools and knowledge, however, as I show in this book, ERM can be utilized in any organizational setting to improve the risk management practices of the organization effectively and efficiently.

The Systematic Review: An Evidence Base for ERM

This book utilizes a broad evidence base on ERM that I gathered through the rigorous systematic review study I conducted for my doctoral research. In this study, I examined the utility of

ERM particularly in relation to complex organizations, using the case study of higher education environments as a frame for analysis. These environments present a wide range of risks that cross multiple organizational boundaries. Traditionally, such institutions had deferred risk management to the individual units most affected by the risks. Such an approach did not look at the overall risk profile of the institution and risks' effects on achieving the institution's strategic objectives. Consequently, higher education leaders had turned to ERM as a strategy to manage institutional risks. However, ERM is a management practice that originated from the corporate sector. This raised the question as to whether an ERM strategy for managing risks was appropriate for higher education. In addition, if an ERM strategy was deemed appropriate for managing risks in higher education, how should leadership implement such a program? Prior to my study, existing ERM frameworks lacked information on how to implement this practice in complex organization settings. Therefore, in my study I posed the following research question: How do critical success factors influence a decision to adopt and implement ERM in higher education institutions? To answer this question, I reviewed both the literature on this topic as well as its connections to academic theories of change management, decision making, and organizational learning. Overall, I showed how these theories could enhance the implementation of ERM in complex organizations—findings I now bring to you. Although the study used higher educational institutions as a framework for analysis, the findings and recommendations from the study are transferable to any organization that has a diverse range of operations, business units, and core functions.

More specifically, in the systematic review, I used a series of study search terms related to ERM to search the electronic database OneSearch for credible scholarly sources on ERM. Initially, the search yielded 999 citations (after duplications were removed). I reviewed all articles in brief (e.g., titles, abstracts, headings) based on the study's inclusion and exclusion criteria. I looked specifically for primary research articles (articles describing research undertaken by the authors themselves) and articles directly relevant to the study's research questions. After this stage, 53 primary studies relevant to the research question remained for review. I then conducted a quality appraisal process to ensure the rigor and validity of the research, which resulted in the further elimination of two studies due to poor quality. I subsequently added four grey literature studies (reports on ERM by organizations), resulting in a final dataset of 55 studies. Figure 1 provides a summary of the results of the search process.

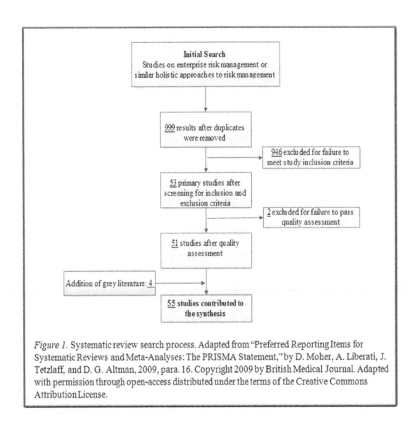

Figure 1. Systematic review search process. Adapted from "Preferred Reporting Items for Systematic Reviews and Meta-Analyses: The PRISMA Statement," by D. Moher, A. Liberati, J. Tetzlaff, and D. G. Altman, 2009, para. 16. Copyright 2009 by British Medical Journal. Adapted with permission through open-access distributed under the terms of the Creative Commons Attribution License.

Several observations can be made of the studies included in the systematic review. First, the studies from peer-reviewed journals included in the dataset were published after 2003, with 84% published after 2009. This highlights that ERM research is still in its infancy. Second, the studies published in peer-reviewed journals were found in the following types of publications: accounting and finance ($n = 19$), risk management and insurance ($n = 14$), engineering ($n = 6$), management sciences ($n = 5$), information technology ($n = 4$), energy management ($n = 2$), and higher education ($n = 1$). These results point to the strong influence the accounting, finance, risk management, and insurance fields have on ERM research. The results also highlight the limited number of studies published in journals dedicated to the management sciences.

As ERM is a global phenomenon, no geographic limitations were placed on the literature reviewed in my study. Consistent with Scott's (1992) assertion that "we can understand much about a specific organization from knowing about other organizations" (p. 1), studies from sectors outside of higher education were also included in the study. This allowed me to observe which ERM implementation mechanisms worked or failed to work across a range of organizational settings. Due to the study's focus on ERM as a high-level framework for managing risk and the challenges of implementing ERM in higher education, technical aspects of risk management were outside the scope of this study. Examples of these include mathematical models for risk assessment and developing   information technology solutions for ERM programs.

Of the studies included in the review, 23 included findings from U.S.-based organizations, while the remaining were from a diverse set of countries and regions including Australia, Brazil, Canada, China, India, Italy, Germany, Malaysia, the Middle East, New Zealand, the Netherlands, Scandinavia, Sri Lanka, Turkey, and Zimbabwe. The studies looked at a wide range of industry sectors, including banking, construction, education, finance, government agencies, insurance, manufacturing, nonprofit organizations, oil and gas, research institutions, services, suppliers, and utilities. These results indicate ERM is a management strategy that has received global attention from a wide variety of industries.

Thirty-five studies employed quantitative methods to analyze data gathered from surveys, controlled studies, or publicly available financial data sources. Twelve studies were qualitative, using methodologies such as case studies and four used mixed methods. Two pieces of grey literature were based on survey findings and two were from roundtables. Hence, research on ERM has been conducted using multiple research methodologies. Last, consistent with the research question this study explored, research on ERM focused on two aspects of ERM: (a) why an organization would adopt ERM and (b) the critical factors that influence ERM implementation. Overall, when looking at the evidence-base as a whole, this book is based on findings from the 55 studies. This entails evidence from 5,614 survey respondents, publicly available data from 935 companies, and data from 35 case studies.

A How-To Guide for ERM

In this book, I provide a detailed overview of ERM, along with a guide for its adoption and implementation. In Part 1, I explain the concepts of organizational risk and risk management in relation to the complex organization, unpacking traditional risk management approaches as well as ERM frameworks in more detail. Then, in Part 2, I review a series of management theories and concepts that can be utilized to enhance understanding and implementation of ERM, including: institutional theory, legitimacy theory, change management models, sensemaking theory, decision sciences, theories of action, absorptive capacity, and organizational resiliency. This is followed in Part 3 by a discussion of factors that affect ERM adoption and implementation. In Part 4, based on my experience as a practitioner tasked with identifying and mitigating risks in his operational unit, and later from my broader role in the University's ERM efforts, I introduce seven principles for ERM adoption and implementation, providing a hands-on tool to guide the ERM process in complex organizational settings. Lastly, in the concluding remarks, I comment to the wide applicability of ERM for complex organizational settings, speaking to the implications of this adopting ERM and areas for future research.

Overall, this book will provide you with both practical and theoretical knowledge for adopting ERM to improve organizational performance. This book expands the body of knowledge on ERM by identifying factors that influence ERM implementation in complex organizational settings, and linking them to a set of management theories that enhance ERM implementation. To date, existing frameworks on ERM have lacked practical information on implementing and integrating ERM across the organization (Fraser, Schoening-Thiessen, & Simkins, 2008). Indeed, a key difference between ERM and traditional risk management practices is that ERM elevates managing risks to a senior leadership level. This entails managing risk across the institution. Therefore, implementing ERM is a broad organizational change initiative.

As a result, this book is useful for senior leadership and risk management practitioners who are seeking evidence-based guidance on how to implement

ERM in their organization. This book addresses the interests of senior leadership by providing answers as to why organizations implement ERM, and the benefits and pitfalls of implementing an ERM program. This book also demonstrates how ERM adoption and implementation—and risk management practices more generally—can be enhanced through the application of theories from management science on change management, decision making, and organizational learning.

Part 1: Understanding Organizational Risk and Risk Management

At its core, adopting and implementing ERM is simply a management process for how an organization identifies and manages risks that threaten achieving its mission and business objects. As such, it entails utilizing sound management practices one would use when implementing a management process in an organization. However, ERM does have distinct elements that practitioners should be aware of when implementing an ERM strategy. Hence, in order to understand how and why ERM may be a good choice for the complex organization, we must first unpack in more detail three key concepts or focus areas that underpin this book: organizational risk, traditional risk management, and ERM. These concepts occur in modern organizational environments that can entail a wide range of structures that may change over time. In addition, such environments often include varying cultural and individual elements such as the culture specific to a nation, organization, or department, or may relate to certain professional disciplines (e.g., teacher, police officer, doctor, accountant, and lawyer). In Part 1, I describe the these three concepts in detail, in order to establish an essential set of knowledge before discussing management theory and practice further in Part 2.

Chapter 1: Organizational Risk

Prior to examining the ERM implementation process, it is necessary to examine why risk presents challenges for complex organizations that necessitate implementing an ERM strategy.

In this chapter, I discuss how the concept of risk has evolved into a critical management function requiring senior leadership attention. I situate risk within the context of the unpredictable, dynamic, and complex business environments in which organizations operate, and how this influences an organization's decision to implement ERM.

Defining Risk

Definitions of risk associated with organizations operating in the modern business environment utilize several unique concepts. For example, Williams, Zainuba, and Jackson (2008) view risk as complex and multidimensional. The authors added that risk is unavoidable, and defined risk from a decision-maker's perspective as

> an assessment of whether an unfavorable outcome might occur (possibility of loss), an assessment of the range of possible unfavorable outcomes (probabilities of such loss),

and an assessment of the extent to which possible unfavorable outcomes can be managed or controlled (exposure to hazard or danger). (Williams et al., 2008, p. 59-60)

A more precise definition of risk is "the uncertainty about outcomes that can be either negative or positive," where risk management is defined as "the process of making and implementing decisions that will minimize the adverse effects of accidental losses to an organization" (Baranoff, Harrington, & Niehaus, 2005, p. 1.4-1.5).

Woon, Azizan, and Samad (2011) proposed three categories of risks that affect an organization's financial performance: (a) tactical risk, which involves the uncertainty of expected earnings; (b) strategic risk, which entails the uncertainty of performance outcomes; and (c) normative risk, which addresses the risk penalty a firm pays for not conducting business within the accepted norms of the industry and society. Similarly, Kaplan and Mikes (2012) proposed a three-category system for classifying organizational risks. First, preventable risks are internal to the organization and arise in the course of business (e.g., safety hazards and improper employee actions). Preventable risks lack strategic benefit but must be actively managed due to the negative impact they can have on the organization. Second,

16

strategic risks are risks a company voluntarily takes in order to generate desired economic returns. Strategic risks are not inherently undesirable but require different strategies to manage than those used to manage preventable risks. Last, external risks surface from outside the organization and are beyond the control of the organization. An organization must develop a process to identify potential external risks and prepare contingency plans to manage them if they occur. These two methodologies for categorizing risks illustrate that not all risks are created equal. Hence, complex organizations need to consider the type of risk when establishing risk assessment strategies and tolerance levels.

Dimensions of Risk

Brinkmann (2013) identified the following six dimensions of risk: measurability, attributability, manageability, insurability, voluntariness, and moral responsibility. Measurability is the quantifiable dimension of risk. Attributability involves whether the risk can be ascribed to organizational decisions. Manageability concerns actions that can prevent or eliminate the risk. Insurability is whether the risk can be insured. Voluntariness deals with whether a risk is chosen using free will and with sufficient knowledge to make an informed decision. Finally, moral responsibility involves whether risk is taken with the informed consent of all parties involved in the decision. Each of Brinkmann's dimensions suggests a certain level of understanding and control an organization has over the risks it faces. However, it is questionable to what extent the complex types of risks modern organizations face are measurable and are under the control of the organization. Moreover, complex organizations need to consider determining the appropriate decision maker(s) for a risk, whether affected people are informed about the risk, and if the financial liability for the risk can be controlled through insurance or other risk transfer mechanisms (e.g., by holding harmless agreements or contracting out the risk exposure).

Risk management processes tend to focus on analyzing risks from an event perspective to determine cause and effect relationships. However, risk is a complex phenomenon, and as Grabowski and Roberts (1997) showed, implementing a risk mitigation system in large organizational settings is difficult. The authors argued that such challenges are related to four characteristics of large systems: (a) simultaneous autonomy and interdependence, (b) intended and unintended consequences, (c) long incubation periods that allow problems to develop, and (d) risk migration. As large systems, complex organizations are likely to encounter these challenges during ERM implementation.

Boisot and McKelvey (2010) used Ashby's law of requisite variety to explain complexity in organizational settings. According to Ashby's law, "only variety can destroy variety" (p. 421). As such, for an organism or social entity to be adaptive, it must be able to match the variety of external stimuli imposed on it. Consequently, the authors proposed that for an organization to be adaptive, it must have a variety of responses available that match the variety of external constraints or threats imposed on the organization. Moreover, when the external variety exceeds the capacity of the organization, adaptive tension develops that seeks to fill the gap between the system's capability and external demands so the system can survive. Consequently, Boisot and McKelvey's (2010) separation of complexity into three regions (chaotic, complex, and ordered) helps explain why certain types of risks can be understood and controlled by the organization, where other risks are more difficult to recognize and comprehend. The chaotic region is typified by stimuli that have no discernible regularities, while the complex region—where most challenges fall—presents some regularity, though it may be difficult to discern. The ordered region involves stimuli that, in theory, can be planned for and controlled.

For example, Andersen (2010) suggested strategic risks can involve significant exposure to organizations due to their high level of uncertainty. Thus, strategic risks often lack easily discernible regularities yet present significant risk to the organization. Hence, strategic risks share the characteristics of the chaotic or complex regions depicted by Boisot and McKelvey (2010). Despite this high exposure level, Andersen (2010) suggested that most risk management approaches tend to focus only on recognized exposures, and are ill-equipped to handle complex risks associated with high levels of uncertainty. This is a particularly salient challenge for ERM since ERM aspires to look at a broad range of organizational risks, including those at the strategic level. However, methodologies for evaluating risks are often based on assessing risks that are more easily identified, measured, and controlled. Examples include risks such as safety hazards or failing to meet regulatory requirements.

Uncertainty and ambiguity can add to the complexity of identifying and understanding an organization's risk exposure. Scott (1992) identified five dimensions of uncertainty. First, the degree of homogeneity/heterogeneity involves the level of diversity of customers and stakeholders an organization must manage. Second, the degree of stability/variability is the extant an organization experiences change. Third, the degree of threat/security concerns how vulnerable an organization is to its environment. Forth, the degree of interconnectedness/ isolation involves how dependent an organization is on other organizations or agencies. Last, the degree of coordination/noncoordination is the extent to which an organization deals with external groups whose actions are coordinated. Due to the diverse set of customers and stakeholders complex organizations regularly interact with and the increasing complexity of the environment in which they operate, the context within which organizations must identify, evaluate, and act on risks also contains a high level of uncertainty. Indeed, Power (2007) stated that "when uncertainty is organized, it becomes a risk to be managed" (p. 6).

The concept of risk is further complicated since leadership involves taking risks and leading organizations through areas where success is not guaranteed (Brinkmann, 2013). March and Shapira (1987) added that leaders often define risk differently than the theoretical literature, and that even two individuals can see the same risk differently. The authors explained that leaders see risk as something they can control, and

21

risk-taking as part of their job and identity as leaders. The authors also found that leaders place more weight on the potential positive outcomes of an activity over negative results. Furthermore, leaders do not see risk as simply a statistical or probability concept, or see value in reducing risk to a single quantifiable measure.

Risk also has social dimensions when situated within the context of an organizational environment. Indeed, Power (2007) suggested risk has "acquired social, political, and organizational significance as never before" (p. 3). Weick (1995) proposed that organizations are networks of people socially interacting through the use of shared meanings and language, and that internal constructions of knowledge are developed in the presence or perceived presence of others. Schein concluded that a social reality consists of the items that groups form consensus around, such as how humans relate to their environment, distribute power, form group boundaries, develop ideology, and share cultural elements. More specific to risk, Argyris (1980) suggested that the inability of organizations to discuss threatening or risky issues is caused by how people are acculturated and socialized (i.e., their values, skills, and action strategies for dealing with challenging issues). Argyris continues that these social elements can inhibit attempts by the organization to encourage employees to disclose information on actions such as unethical behavior or hazardous working conditions. Consequently, organizations must manage a diverse set of risks that require different means to assess and control. Moreover, individual backgrounds and perceptions on risks and the organizational environment influences how an organization evaluates and responds to risk.

Risk and Opportunity

Enterprise risk management implies that effectively managing risk can result in improving an organization's ability to recognize and capitalize on opportunity. Arnold, Benford, Canada, and Sutton (2011) conceived of ERM as having either a defensive focus on risk control and avoidance or an offensive focus that looks at the upside of risk in order to identify opportunities the organization can exploit. Arnold, Benford, Hampton, and Sutton (2012) made a similar argument that as ERM programs mature, they increase their ability to manage risks and opportunity. Indeed, Power (2007) argued that organizations that are more effective at aligning their business strategy with organizational governance, regulatory compliance, and enterprise goals will be better positioned to realize opportunities that emerge. Hence, it is logical to conclude that an organization's leadership would be more likely to implement ERM if the program also enhances the organization's ability to identify and act on opportunities.

Brunswicker and Hutschek (2010) predicted that firms that use active processes for identifying opportunities from external and distant sources will be more successful at finding potentially exploitable opportunities. Similarly, Baron and Ensley (2006) defined opportunity recognition as "the process through which ideas for potentially profitable new business ventures are identified by specific persons" (p. 1331). Riquelme (2013) identified three factors that influence a person's ability to recognize opportunities: cognitive frameworks, self-efficacy, and social networks. The decision on whether to exploit an opportunity is dependent on attitudes toward the opportunity (favorable or unfavorable view of the opportunity), subjective norms (peer pressure on whether or not to act on the opportunity), and perceived behavioral control (perceived ease of difficulty to exploit the opportunity successfully). Opportunities that are favorably perceived in these areas are more likely to be acted on than those that are viewed less favorably in one or more of these dimensions (De Jong, 2013). As such, the ability to identify opportunities

24

is influenced by individual and social dynamics similar to those associated with identifying risks. Moreover, assessing whether the organization should act on the opportunity should also include evaluating the risks associated with the opportunity. Hence, organizations can integrate risk identification and assessment processes with opportunity identification processes so that each compliments and strengths the other.

In sum, risk is a complex phenomenon that has multiple dimensions. As such, a one-size-fits-all strategy for evaluating and managing risks is unlikely to be successful. Consequently, the complexity and multiple dimensions of risks warrant managing risks using a holistic approach as offered by ERM. Moreover, an organization's capability to identify and control risks effectively is linked with its ability to capitalize on opportunities.

Chapter 2: Traditional Risk Management

Now that we have an understanding of organizational risk more generally, we can look at the different types of risk management that ultimately may lead an organization to adopt an ERM program. In this chapter, I review the concept of traditional risk management, which serves as a basis to then understand the ERM framework presented in the following chapter.

Traditional risk management is defined as "the process of making and implementing decisions that will minimize the adverse effects of accidental losses on an organization" (Baranoff et al., 2005, p. 1.5). This approach to risk management aims to identify potential loss exposures and examine the feasibility of various strategies to limit these exposures (Baranoff et al., 2005). Strategies utilized to manage risks fall into two categories: risk control and risk finance. According to Baranoff et al. (2005), there are six core risk control techniques: "avoidance, loss prevention, loss reduction, separation, duplication, and diversification" (p. 2.19). As the name implies, avoidance simply means the organization does not take on an activity that exposes it to certain risks. Loss prevention and reduction involve actions to reduce the frequency and severity of losses from risks. Separation entails splitting up assets so they are

26

not all exposed to the same risk. Duplication involves the use of redundant systems to prevent the shutdown of an operation or process. Finally, diversification spreads risk exposures over a range of operations, markets, or geographic regions. Examples of risk finance techniques include transfer methods, such as insurance, hold-harmless agreements, and hedging; while an example of retention is the self-funding of losses (Baranoff et al., 2005).

Traditional risk management techniques fail to address the full range of risk exposures a complex organization may face. Arena, Arnaboldi, and Azzone (2011) argued that a limit of traditional risk management is its tendency to manage risk categories separately. Traditional risk management functions have often been located in the accounting, financial, compliance, and internal auditor areas of organizations (Blaskovich & Taylor, 2011). Moreover, March and Shapira (1987) contended that theories on managerial perspectives of risk, such as classical decision theory, oversimplify human behavior and thus do not accurately explain how managers perceive risk. Brinkmann (2013) suggested that the complexity of modern risk combined with increased pressure to hold organizations accountable for their actions can lead to managers focusing on providing a defendable justification for their decisions concerning risk at the expense of using sound professional judgment. Accordingly, Brinkmann (2013) posited the need for "intelligent risk management" based on the following tenets: (a) control systems that are not allowed to overburden managerial attention and innovation, (b) higher tolerance levels for disorganization and ambiguity in the risk management process, and (c) internal control systems that focus on generating usable knowledge and that are always challengeable. Enterprise risk management frameworks such as the one offered by COSO begin to address the three dimensions of intelligent risk management; however, they require more insight on how to manage risks without stifling innovation, how to assess risks with high levels of ambiguity, and how to create actionable knowledge through the risk management process.

In sum, modern organizations face a wide range of complex risks that challenge their ability to meet mission-critical objectives. In addition, managing risk is more complicated in large institutions composed of multiple subunits that operate in a global, changing economy (Grabowski & Roberts, 1997). Within the complex institution, the failure to manage risks properly can lead to events that challenge an organization's ability to meet critical objectives and jeopardize its survival. As McShane et al. (2011) stated, "Managing risks has become a

28

critical function for CEOs as organizational environments become increasingly turbulent and complex" (p. 653). A survey by North Carolina State University and Protiviti (2015) identified the top risks executives perceive their organizations face as regulatory changes, economic conditions that restrict growth, attracting and retain talent, inability to identify risks, cyber threats, managing unexpected crisis, sustaining customer loyalty, resistance to change that restricts the ability adjust business models, and not meeting performance expectations. Consequently, in light of these issues, traditional approaches to risk management should be replaced by methods that position risk management as part of an organization's governance process, allowing for a more holistic view of the organization's risk exposure. Enterprise risk management is such a strategy.

Chapter 3: Frameworks for ERM

There are several existing frameworks for ERM, including: the Casualty Actuarial Society ERM framework, the COSO ERM integrated framework, the International Organization for Standardization (ISO) 31,000 risk management framework and process, the Australian and New Zealand standard for risk management, and the Federation of European Risk Management Associations' risk management standard (Andersen, 2010; Kimbrough & Componation, 2009). These frameworks share similar risk management steps and highlight how ERM influences a broad range of activities and organizational levels (Kimbrough & Componation, 2009). Moreover, these frameworks portray ERM as a top-down, driven risk management approach (Andersen, 2010). In this chapter, I present the COSO ERM integrated framework, which provides a basis for the discussion throughout this book, since it is the most prevalent model referenced in the literature.

In 1985, COSO was established to address the increased incidence of fraudulent financial reporting. This initially resulted in COSO developing frameworks to improve financial reporting and compliance, followed by the publication of the ERM integrated framework in 2004, which is referenced by several U.S. and international standard-setting bodies (Landsittel & Rittenberg, 2010). The committee is composed of five sponsoring organizations: the American Accounting Association, the American Institute of Certified Public Accountants, Financial Executives International, the Institute of Internal Auditors, and the Institute of Management Accountants. Its mission is "to provide thought leadership through the development of comprehensive frameworks and guidance on enterprise risk management, internal control, and fraud deterrence designed to improve organizational performance and governance and to reduce the extent of fraud in organizations" (Landsittel & Rittenberg, 2010, p. 457). The committee's composition and mission are especially important as they reveal the professional background of the framework's developers and, subsequently, the challenges organizations may have implementing a framework that relies heavily on internal controls and top-down management strategies.

According to COSO (2004), enterprise risk management is a process, affected by an entity's board of directors, management and other personnel, applied in strategy setting across the enterprise, designed to identify potential events that may affect the entity, and manage risk to be within its risk appetite, to provide reasonable assurance   regarding   the achievement of entity objectives. (p. 4)

This definition outlines the following six key elements of ERM: (a) led by senior management, (b) integrated throughout the organization, (c) considers risk from a strategic perspective, (d) provides reasonable assurance of meeting an organization's goals, (e) identifies risks that affect the organization, and (f) manages risk based on the organization's risk appetite and tolerance level. In addition, COSO proposed four critical areas for establishing risk management objectives: (a) strategic objectives, which involve high-level goals and the mission of the organization; (b) operation objectives, which outline the efficient use of organizational resources; (c) objectives to meet an organization's reporting requirements; and (d) regulatory compliance objectives. According to COSO (2004), organizations need to set objectives for managing risk at each organizational level to include the entity, divisional, business unit, and subsidiary levels of the organization.

The COSO (2004) ERM framework is composed of eight interrelated components. These include: (a) the internal environment, such as the organization's risk management philosophy, ethical values, and the operating environment; (b) objectives that align with the organization's tolerance for risk; (c) the identification of internal and external events that present risks to the organization; (d) the assessment of events to determine the likelihood and impact risks may have on the organization; (e) the selection of responses to control risks, such as avoiding, accepting, reducing, or sharing the risk; (f) the establishment of control activities, such as policies and procedures to help ensure risks are adequately addressed; (g) the adoption of mechanisms to communicate and capture information on risks; and (h) the implementation of processes to assess and monitor the state of the ERM program continually. Figure 2 illustrates the basic logic of the COSO framework. Here, risk objectives are set in their respective domains for each level of the organization, and realized through the application of the eight interrelated components. Although portrayed in the illustration as a linear operation, the process is, in practice, more iterative with activities co-occurring across each area.

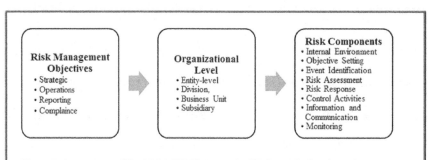

Figure 2. Components of the COSO ERM framework. This figure depicts the main components and subelements of the COSO ERM framework (adapted from COSO, 2004, p. 23). Used with permission from the American Institute of Certified Public Accountants.

In sum, the COSO framework reflects practices found in mechanistic organizational settings typified by management practices that focus on control and top-down decision making. Mikes (2009) described this framework as advocating for ERM as a "strategic management control system" (p. 20). Consequently, the framework provides limited information on managing risks in global, multiorganizational, large-scale systems with diverse management processes led by a wide variety of people (Grabowski & Roberts, 1997). Formal approaches to risk management such as these may lead to a focus on identifiable and quantifiable risks instead of the strategic risks that have more uncertainty (Andersen, 2010). Indeed, Fraser, Schoening-Thiessen, and Simkins (2008) found that executives expressed concern over the lack of information on integrating ERM across their organizations, and viewed the framework as impractical to implement.

In addition, ERM is a relatively new practice. The first evidence of such activity occurred in 1998, with the first academic study on ERM published in 1999 by Colquitt, Hoyt, and Lee. In this initial study, Colquitt et al. investigated the role risk managers have in nonoperational risks and the techniques they use to control these risks. Subsequently, the majority of research on ERM has been published in peer-reviewed insurance and accounting journals (Iyer, Rogers, & Simkins, 2010), and tends to favor quantitative approaches to risk analysis and the use of management control systems. Landsittel and Rittenberg (2010) have argued that ERM research needs to go deeper than simple assessments of current best practices. Iyer et al. (2010) further stated that ERM research lacks a natural "disciplinary home" and, as such, is a topic that can be studied from a variety of management theory perspectives (p. 420). As such, in Part 2, I explore how concepts from the management sciences in areas such as change management, decision making, and organizational learning can advance understanding on ERM from both practical and theoretical perspectives.

Part 2: Management Science and ERM:

From Theory to Practice

In Part 1, I discussed the key concepts of organizational risk, traditional risk management, and the COSO ERM framework. One of the key findings from my research is that knowledge on ERM implementation has been disconnected from management concepts, despite its clear connection to senior leadership and management strategy. This is true both of research on ERM as well as in how it is practically implemented in organizations. Therefore, in order to provide a comprehensive understanding of ERM, in Part 2, I review concepts in management science theory that may enhance ERM implementation within complex organizations (see Figure 3). In the chapters that follow, I focus on three main areas: organizational change, decision making, and organizational learning. For each area, I first explain aspects of the theories more generally, followed by how that area connects to the COSO ERM framework.

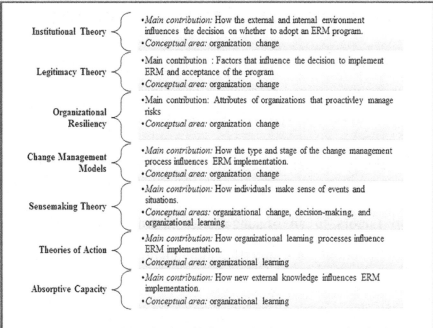

Figure 3. Management science theories. This figure depicts key management theories discussed in Part 2, their main contribution, and the conceptual areas to which they are linked.

37

Chapter 4: Organizational Change I –

Institutional Theory, Legitimacy Theory,

and Organizational Culture

Concepts relating to institutional theory, legitimacy theory, and organizational culture can be used to analyze how external and internal factors in an organization's environment influence the decision to adopt ERM and the implementation process. In this chapter, I unpack these models to provide a context to understand change management more generally.

Institutional Theory

Institutional theory speaks to how external pressures from governmental agencies, laws and regulations, stakeholders, professional norms, and the public influence an organization (Wicks, 2001). Scott (2014) explained that "institutions comprise regulative, normative, and cultural cognitive elements that, together with associated activities and resources, provide stability and meaning to social life" (p. 56). Moreover, he proposed that each element operates through distinct mechanisms and forms the "three pillars of institutional theory," which are: (a) regulative, which focuses on expedience, coercive mechanisms, and regulative rules; (b) normative, which relies on social obligation, normative mechanisms, and binding expectations; and (c) culture-cognitive, which values shared understanding, mimetic mechanisms, and cultural influences. These elements help to provide institutions with the meaning and stability that create organizational structures and guide behavior.

However, each has distinct underlying assumptions and mechanisms that can be used as analytical elements for understanding institutions. More specifically, the regulative element focuses on expedience, coercive mechanisms, and regulative rules; the normative component relies on social obligation, normative mechanisms, and binding expectations; and the culture-cognitive element values shared understanding and mimetic mechanisms. Consequently, institutional theory is used to analyze how an organization's history, culture, and operating environment shape the decision to adopt ERM and influence the type of program implemented.

Legitimacy Theory

Suchman (1995) defined legitimacy as "a generalized perception or assumption that the actions of an entity are desirable, proper, or appropriate within some socially constructed system of norms, values, beliefs, and definitions" (p. 574). Suchman (1995) also asserted that there are three broad types of organizational legitimacy: pragmatic, moral, and cognitive. Pragmatic legitimacy relates to whether the activity is perceived as beneficial to the organization and its stakeholders. Thomas and Lamm (2012) stated that such perceived benefits may include items such as better use of resources, reduced risk and legal liability, and improved reputation; items similar to those benefits touted by ERM proponents. Secondly, Suchman (1995) argued that legitimacy has a moral dimension that involves whether an organization's actions and image are consistent with socially accepted norms. This moral legitimacy includes beliefs stakeholders share about an activity's value in advancing the interests of society. However, Suchman (1995) cautioned that resistance and organizational politics can significant affect moral legitimacy. Lastly, cognitive legitimacy involves how easily an activity is comprehended and how consistent it is with existing organizational culture and belief system. Here, people assess whether the activity will make their job easier or more difficult (Thomas & Lamm, 2012).

Protecting and enhancing the organization's identity can also have positive effects on the overall perceptions members have of the organization. For example, people develop their personal identities in part through their perception of how others view the organization where they work (Weick, 1995). Indeed, Ravasi and Schultz (2006) found that how people perceive identity threats to an organization is influenced by how they believe the organization is perceived externally and their assumptions about the distinctive behavioral patterns of the organization. The authors also found that organizational responses to identity threats can be limited by the need to reconcile responses with external changes. Moreover, the organization's culture provides the context for the sensemaking process the organization undergoes as it seeks to understand, reevaluate, and redefine the organization in response to the identity threat.

Within the context of complex organizations, the reasons organizations adopt a new business practice such as ERM can vary. For example, Gioia and Thomas (1996) found measures like profit and return are not as relevant to higher education leadership. Instead, items such as prestige and ranking are critical, making an institution's image a critical strategic issue. According to the authors, leadership issues can be separated into two categories: strategic and political. Strategic issues are items associated with creating the desired future

41

state, while political issues involve the status quo and managing competing interests. The authors found that image and identity powerfully influence how leaders in organizations interpret the critical issues they confront and that strategy and information processing are critical to how leaders interpret these issues. Consequently, the literature suggests that organizational leadership will be moved to adopt ERM when leadership sees linkage between adopting ERM and protecting and enhancing the institution's reputation. Legitimacy theory thus addresses the issue of why a certain course of action is accepted by an organization and hence helps explain the factors that influence whether members of the organization accept an initiative such as ERM (Suchman, 1995). Therefore, legitimacy theory is used to explain the logic for why leadership at a complex organization may select an ERM strategy and factors that affect employee perceptions on the validity of the program.

Organizational Culture

Mintzberg and Westley (1992) posited that changing an organization's culture involves shifting the collective mindset of the organization. On the other hand, Schein (2010) proposed that culture is formed as organizations solve problems of external adaption and internal integration, such as an organization's mission, strategy, goals, and methods to measure progress. Internal integration problems include creating a common language and defining group boundaries, power distribution, and behavioral norms. Schein (2010) added that an organization's overall culture is influenced by national and ethnic identities, cultures from other organizations with which the organization interacts, cultures associated with different occupations, and microcultures that develop in cross-functional organizational groups. He found that these cultural forces are powerful and significantly affect the actions of the organization. Schein (2010) also argued that an organization's culture is, in part, a "learned defense mechanism to avoid uncertainty," which can cause the organization to fail to address uncertainty proactively (p. 277). Lastly, Schein stated that a concern for an organization's culture is an issue unique to leadership and one that differentiates leadership from general management and administration. Based on Schein's broader definition of organizational culture, Cooper, Faseruk, and Kahn (2013) defined risk culture as

> a pattern of basic assumptions that the group learned as it identified, evaluated,

and managed its internal and external risks that has worked well enough to be considered valid, and therefore to be taught to new members as the correct way to perceive, think, and feel in relation to those risks. (p. 65)

As Cooper's definition of risk culture illuminates, developing a risk culture at a complex organization entails building the organization's understanding of how it identifies, understands, and manages risks. Therefore, leadership plays a critical role in ERM programs that aspire to change the culture surrounding how the institution understands and responds to risks.

As further discussed in relation to decision making, Osland and Bird (2000) utilized the concept of sensemaking to help explain how people understand different cultures. In particular, they explored cultural paradoxes where situations cause different and contradictory responses. The authors stressed the need for context to understand actions and responses in a cultural setting. They further determined that cultural values and histories influence the schema people select in a situation. They defined a schema as "a pattern of social interaction that is characteristic of a particular cultural group" (p. 71). Indeed, Schein (1993) warned that complex business and societal problems are often caused by cultural misunderstandings.   These

44

issues can be amplified in complex organizational settings with multiple cultural elements. Therefore, understanding how diverse cultural units and associated views on risk affect ERM implementation is critical, worthy of deeper exploration, and directly related to the internal environment COSO speaks to in its ERM framework.

For example, at universities and colleges, Birnbaum (1988) noted the cultural divide between faculty and administrators, where faculty viewed administrators as imposing red tape and constraints on their work, and administrators viewed faculty as unconcerned with costs and reasonable appeals for accountability. To address the different priorities between faculty and administrators, Birnbaum suggested that HEIs have two distinct control structures: one for administrative decisions and another for faculty. Birnbaum (1988) also explained there are four basic models for how HEIs function: collegial, bureaucratic, political, and anarchical. As the name implies, collegial institutions value shared power and consensus with leadership that seeks input on decisions, and where responsibility is collectively shared. However, Birnbaum noted that collegial institutions only work for relatively small organizational settings. In contrast, a bureaucratic institution is common to colleges in which large-scale

45

administrative functions are organized to reduce uncertainty and improve performance. In this setting, people can be more easily replaced and are not as critical to the overall performance of the institution (e.g., in community colleges where faculty only teach part-time). On the other hand, faculty members at political institutions are deeply connected to the organization and are often part of a wide array of specialized subunits. Consequently, such an organization is too complex for a bureaucratic structure and thus relies on decentralized decision making with diffused power. This results in constant competition among subunits for resources and influence on the direction of the organization. Lastly, anarchical institutions are characterized by having several schools or units that appear to operate independently from the overall organization. Anarchical institutions often have vague goals, ambiguous understandings of how inputs are converted to outputs, and unclear decision-making processes. Consequently, from a broad perspective, there are unique cultures at universities and colleges that require adapting the ERM process so it is compatible with the existing culture and management style at the institution.

Chapter 5: Organizational Change II – Change Management

Theories on change management can be used to analyze how to implement a broad organizational initiative such as ERM. Therefore, in this chapter, I explain change management and models for change management within the context of the complex organization. Change requires leaders to manage the interests of diverse and vast groups of stakeholders (Jongbloed, Enders, & Salerno, 2008). According to Kezar and Eckel (2002), strategies for transformational change at complex organizations include leadership support, collaboration, well-designed programs, staff development, and observable action. The authors found that these strategies are effective because they provide opportunities for key stakeholders to help create direction and priorities for change, clarify roles, and understand what change means for them. The authors pointed out that the real value of such strategies is their ability to generate organizational sensemaking.

Gioia and Chittipeddi (1991) studied a major change initiative at a large public university. The authors defined change as an effort to alter how an organization thinks and acts, and strategic change as organizational

47

change that seeks to capitalize on critical opportunities and respond to potential threats. The authors concluded that change requires organizational members to make sense of the organization's internal and external environment, and to understand change in relation to their existing cognitive interpretation of what the change initiative means for them. Gioia, Thomas, Clark, and Chittipeddi (1994) also conducted research on strategic change. They found that task forces that are charged with implementing change go through four stages. First, people interpret who they are, their responsibilities for the change initiative, and what external forces influence their ability to act. Next, members of the task force define their role in the change initiative and determine the methods for implementing the initiative. The group then moves to the legitimation stage, which focuses on how to enhance the organization's perception of the group as legitimate agents for the change initiative. Last, the task force works to increase its influence in an effort to institutionalize change so it has a lasting impact on the organization. Hence, complex organizations that choose to use a team for ERM implementation should select members who can be effective at guiding the program through the strategic change process.

Woon et al. (2011) posited that ERM is a change management initiative that requires a significant shift in an organization's mindset about managing risk. However, Schein (2010) cautioned that leaders must first understand the general process for organizational change before attempting to change the culture of an organization. In keeping with these findings, the literature on change management has identified key elements of the organizational change process. For example, Cinite et al. (2009) identified factors that indicate whether an organization is ready for change (e.g., senior management's commitment, competent change agents, and immediate managers' support). According to the authors, employees desire competent change champions that consider options prior to implementing change, a senior management team that is decisive about an organization's strategies and goals for change, and leadership that is committed to the success of the change initiative. In addition, employees desire managers that encourage participation in change, share information, and acknowledge the impact of change on people. Cinite, Duxbury, and Higgins (2009) also found that factors indicative of a lack of readiness for change include poor communication of the reasons for and benefits of the change

49

initiative, increased workloads, and workloads that do not allow employees to participate in the change initiative.

Change Management Models

Organizational change is defined by Van de Ven and Poole (1995) as "a difference in form, quality, or state over time in an organizational entity" (p. 512). Kurt Lewin, a social scientist that studied how to resolve social conflict, forged understanding of organizational change through his development of a 3-step model for change based on unfreezing existing behaviors, moving (learning) new behaviors, and refreezing new behaviors by making them congruent with the environment (Burnes, 2004). Schein (2010) further elaborated on Lewin's work by proposing a conceptual model for managed cultural change. Consistent with Lewin's theory on change, Schein (2010) proposed that change consists of three stages: unfreezing, changing, and refreezing. The unfreezing stage entails creating the motivation to change by using information to challenge existing beliefs. This is paired with the creation of survival anxiety to motivate change, and psychological safety to overcome learning anxiety. The changing stage takes place by learning new concepts, meanings, and standards for judgment. This stage is aided by providing role

50

models with whom people can identify and fostering opportunities to pursue new solutions and for trial-and-error learning. The refreezing stage involves internalizing these new concepts, meanings, and standards, and incorporating them into self-conception and identity, and ongoing relationships. Such organizational change models were used to examine how the type and stage of the change management process influences ERM implementation. Orlikowski and Hofman (1997) add that organizational change is a dynamic ongoing process involving multiple stages of change interacting in an iterative manner. The authors referred to this as the improvisational model for managed change that "recognizes that change is typically an ongoing process made up of opportunities and challenges that are not necessarily predictable at the start" (p. 13). Theoretical work on change management provides a means to clarify the process of implementing an organizational-wide initiative such as ERM and the challenges likely to be encountered in such an endeavor.

Mintzberg and Westley (1992) explained how organizational change occurs at different levels in an organization. In this model, the highest level of change occurs in an organization's culture and vision, followed by changes in structure and positions, systems and programs, and people and facilities. Mintzberg and Westley (1992) argued that changing an organization's culture and vision must include change at the lower levels. Similarly, Schein (2010) stated that embedding mechanisms for cultural change fall into two categories. The first category entails primary embedding mechanisms such as what leadership pays attention to, measures and controls, how leaders react to critical events or crises, how resources and rewards are allocated, intentional role modeling and coaching, and how people are recruited, selected, and promoted. Schein referred to the other category as secondary articulation and reinforcement mechanisms that include items such as organizational structure and procedures, rituals, building design and layout, stories regarding important organizational events, and formal statements and creeds.

Orlikowski and Hofman (1997) proposed that change is an ongoing process that involves three different types of change that build on each other in an iterative manner: anticipated, emergent, and opportunity-based. Anticipated change is planned for and happens as designed, while emergent change occurs suddenly, was not intended, and is generated by local innovation. Opportunity-based change is not planned but implemented in response to opportunities that arise while the change initiative is being implemented. The authors noted that this type of change requires flexibility and that management's role should be focused on guiding change, not controlling it. Furthermore, employees responsible for change must be provided the responsibility, resources, and ability to influence the change process.

Chapter 6: Organizational Change III – Organizational Control and Resilience

Various ERM frameworks propose implementing organizational control mechanisms to manage risks. Therefore, understanding organizational control and resilience—the concepts featured in this chapter—is important to understanding organizational change more broadly. Simon (1994) defined organizational control systems as the recognized information-driven routines and practices used to sustain or change organizational activities. He specified four types of organizational control systems: (a) belief systems, which top management uses to communicate direction and purpose; (b) boundary systems, which set limits for the organization and its members; (c) diagnostic control systems, which generate feedback for monitoring outcomes; and (d) interactive control systems, which top managers use to inject themselves into the decision-making process of subordinates. Simon (1994) found that new managers use control systems to overcome organizational complacency, communicate new agendas, establish implementation objectives and timelines, focus attention through incentives, and concentrate organizational learning on addressing the uncertainty of the new direction. Consequently, control systems—when used effectively—can be powerful tools for communicating organizational goals and boundaries, and can assist in creating commitment and shared beliefs for organizational activities.

Weick (1995) outlined three levels of control in an organization: (a) first-order control, which entails direct supervision; (b) second-order control, which involves programs and routine activities; and (c) third-order control, which is based on assumptions that are taken for granted by organization members. Weick (1995) explained that first- and second-order controls require that the work is understood by the organization and affected employees and is sub dividable in order for controls, rules, and standardized procedures to work effectively. Weick (1995) also specified that third-order controls are more important at the top of organizations where nonroutine work is common. However, third-order controls are highly influenced by personal and cultural biases that can result in defensive and self-justifying behavior. Therefore, challenges may arise with using control systems in organizations. For example, faculty members with significant freedom to conduct non-routine research activities may oppose imposing controls on them. Hence, complex organizations may encounter resistance implementing first- or second-order control systems for non-routine research while the application of third order controls may be hindered due to the personal preferences of faculty.

Organizational Resilience

Despite efforts to address risk, organizations need to have the capacity to respond to crises that develop from the residual and inherent risks of conducting business. For example, Williams et al. (2008) noted that risk is unavoidable and exists only when uncertainty exists about a positive outcome. Similarly, Roberts and Bea (2001) pointed out that any complex and interdependent system will eventually fail, and thus organizations must plan for such occasions. However, this does not mean organizations should not take proactive steps to prevent these breakdowns. Therefore, organizational resilience is used to explain how complex organizations can prepare for the adverse events that affect the institution. Resilient organizations actively try to understand what they do not know, and communicate the larger picture of the organization's mission and employees' roles in fulfilling that mission (Roberts & Bea, 2001). In addition, resilient organizations utilize multiple and diverse decision-making methods and focus on developing shared mental models to mitigate risk (Grabowski & Roberts, 1997).

Weick (2011) proposed that resilient organizations expect interruptions to operations, take steps to identify the impacts of failure, and create early warning signs that indicate potential failure points. Roberts and Bea (2001) found that critical characteristics of high-reliability organizations include aggressively trying to know what they do not know, utilizing a balanced reward and incentive plan that looks at costs from a long-term perspective, and ensuring everyone understands the big picture and their role in realizing this vision. Therefore, organizations need to plan for organizational crises that may occur due to residual risk; that is, the risk that remains after risk response actions have been implemented as part of the ERM program.

In another study, Bigley and Roberts (2001) examined the Incident Command System used at a large California fire department to determine what attributes of the system could be applied to organizations facing complex and ambiguous situations. The Incident Command System is a management system agencies use to respond to emergencies. It is both highly structured and flexible. Based on their findings, the authors proposed that organizations that face potential situations that require a reliable and error-free response develop a temporary system to manage these situations. This system should be based on the following: preplanned design structures and response guidelines, methods to develop and maintain mental models during the response, discouragement of uncoordinated or *ad lib* responses; training and development programs; and after-action reviews. Such a program should be developed in a manner that integrates resources across the entity. Consequently, ERM can help an organization's planning process for emergencies by capturing and sharing critical information on the risks the institution faces. Incorporation of such information into the organization's emergency training and exercise initiatives can aid in facilitating organizational learning on both the risks the organization faces and its emergency response process and capabilities.

Moreover, resilient organizations provide a roadmap of a culture that captures the essence of organizations that effectively manage risk. For example, Weick and Sutcliffe (2007) propose that resilient organizations have five characteristics. First, they have a preoccupation with failure. Resilient organizations encourage reporting errors and use failures as an opportunity to learn how to improve processes. Second, they are reluctant to accept simplification. Instead, they take active steps to thoroughly understand the risks the organization faces and value diverse expertise and opinions. Third, resilient organizations are sensitive to operations. This allows them to develop situational awareness through a dedication to understanding the challenges front line personnel confront. Fourth, they are committed to resilience. This entails a willingness to acknowledge that no system is perfect and thus they constantly seek to identify and learn from errors and/or failures. Last, they have deference to expertise. Resilient organizations push decision-making authority out to the people who are the most knowledgeable of the process, regardless of their position in the organization. Consequently, complex organizations should look to develop these cultural dimensions as part of the ERM program, especially in operations that present significant, complex risks such developing new industrial technologies.

In sum, critical findings from the literature related to change management are: (a) designing the program to reflect the organization's culture, (b) ERM implementation as a significant organizational change initiative, (c) implementation as a dynamic and ongoing process, (d) long-term commitment to implementing ERM, and (e) ERM as means to build organizational resiliency. Hence changing the culture at an organization is a long, ongoing, complex process. To improve the acceptability of ERM at the early stages of implementation, the organization should design the program to be compatible with the existing culture and practices at the organization. Achieving the long-term goal of improving the risk management culture at the institution requires understanding ERM as a long-term process that is ongoing and dynamic in nature. Hence, the ERM program will need to be continually adapted to the new realities and challenges encountered throughout implementation. Last, the attributes of resilient organizations can form the basis for the attributes of an effective risk management culture. Thus, organizations should seek to build organizational resiliency by implementing ERM.

Chapter 7: Organizational Change and COSO's ERM Framework

With our new understanding of the broader concepts of organizational change, in this chapter I show how these concepts relate to the implementation of ERM in the complex organization. The literature suggests implementing a significant organizational initiative such as ERM at a complex organization is a complex process requiring leadership commitment. To affect change requires that leadership understand the process of change and whether the organization is ready for change. Therefore, the complexity and diverse cultures found at complex organizations necessitate that a change initiative such as ERM be designed and implemented in a manner that is consistent with management theories on organizational change. The findings further highlight the difficulty organizations may encounter when implementing an ERM program that aspires to change existing practices at the institution. Hence, an organization should first consider designing the ERM program to fit the culture and management practices at the institution. Starting with an ERM program that recognizes the existing institutional cultural and practices should reduce the initial level of organization change needed to launch the program. However, organizations should not neglect that the long-term object of ERM is to integrate risk management into the institution's management practices. Therefore, consistent with the change models, organizations need to determine the ERM program goals for each organizational level and establish mechanisms for embedding risk management into the institution's management practices.

In sum, organizational change entails the environment conditions at the organization that influence ERM implementation. Hence, the organizational change area involves the internal environment, objective setting, and internal control components of the COSO ERM framework. An organization's internal environment includes items such as the history and culture of the organization, its risk management philosophy, the level of risk it is comfortable accepting, its ethical values, its organizational structure, and how it distributes authority (COSO, 2004). The objective setting component requires objectives to be aligned with an organization's risk appetite and tolerance levels (COSO, 2004).

Risk appetite is the balance the organization chooses between growth, risk, and return; and risk tolerance is the level of variation it accepts to achieve its objectives (COSO, 2004, p. 20). To accomplish this, an organization must evaluate the risks associated with the strategic objectives the organization sets to achieve its mission and vision. Moreover, strategic objectives are used as the basis for establishing risk management objectives in areas such as operations, reporting, and compliance. The COSO (2004) framework also includes control activities to ensure the organization's exposure to risk is kept within the tolerance limits set by the organization. Control activities involve establishing and implementing policies and procedures that outline risk management activities at all levels of the organization. Examples include requiring preapproval, authorizations, verifications, assessing operations, and the segregation of duties.

Several authors have found evidence to support COSO's (2004) assertion that ERM needs to speak to an organization's internal environment and objective-setting process. For example, Gates, Nicolas, and Walker's (2012) survey of risk management executives from companies with ERM programs suggested that improvements in an organization's internal environment builds management consensus, leads to better decision making, and creates higher levels of accountability for the ERM program. In addition, Cooper et al.'s (2013) meta-analysis of existing ERM literature found organizational culture can be either a major benefit or a major barrier to ERM implementation. However, the authors found only limited support for the "tone at the top" impact on understanding and controlling risk. Furthermore, they found that defining an organization's risk appetite improves the ability to manage risk.

A key element of COSO's (2004) objective-setting process involves integrating risk management into the process an organization uses to establish its strategic objectives. In addition, the risks associated with strategic objectives are evaluated and used as a basis for gauging risk in other areas, such as operations, reporting, and compliance. Throughout this process, risks are identified in each area and assessed based on the organization's risk appetite and tolerance (COSO, 2004). In this regard, Louisot and Ketcham (2009) stated that ERM improves an organization's strategic decision making by integrating discussions on threats and opportunities into the strategic planning process. Similarly, COSO (2004) stresses the importance of understanding and developing risk management objectives for each organizational level.

Kimbrough and Componation (2009) noted that the major frameworks for ERM implementation (i.e., Casualty Actuarial Society ERM framework, COSO ERM integrated framework, and ISO 31,000 risk management framework and process) all suggest culture change as a primary concern with ERM implementation. However, these frameworks provide limited guidance on the impact culture has on ERM implementation, or how to change an organization's culture to improve the ERM implementation processes. Moreover, the authors posited that existing frameworks portray ERM implementation in a manner that reflects only mechanistic organizational cultures. Mechanistic cultures are characterized by controlling management who believe employees need detailed direction and coercion to act for the organization. This raises a concern that ERM is viewed as needing to change the organization's culture versus the organization adopting ERM to fit with the existing culture. For example, implementing an ERM strategy that relies heavily on quantifying risks and control mechanisms may fit the culture at a financial firm while not holding relevance for the culture at a complex institutions.

In regards to theory, although the COSO (2004) ERM framework refers to normative and culture-cognitive elements, the framework relies heavily on the regulative element outlined in institutional theory. Thus, the framework lacks insight on key mechanisms that enable organizations to build shared understandings on how they manage risk. Institutions with diverse organizational cultures require an ERM framework that reflects the existing institutional forces that

65

drive action in each subculture of the organization. Moreover, the ERM framework should recognize how the organization's existing assumptions and behaviors influence ERM effectiveness.

Lastly, Beasley, Clune, and Hermanson's (2005) research on ERM implementation in the banking, education, and insurance industries found that senior management and board of directors' leadership were the most critical factors for ERM implementation. Kleffner et al. (2003) found that that key deterrents to ERM implementation are organizational structure, culture, resistance to change, and lack of qualified personnel to implement ERM. In addition, Yaraghi and Langhe (2011) concluded that having a well-defined and clear long-term strategy for risk management is the most critical element in ERM implementation. Consequently, ERM touches on key strategic issues at a complex organization such as its risk management philosophy and culture, and the institution's strategic objectives. Moreover, as an organizational initiative that aspires to affect how the organization thinks about and manages its risks, ERM requires the attention and commitment of senior leadership.

Chapter 8: Decision Making I –

Sensemaking Theory

Moving to the second of the three main concepts reviewed in Part 2, in this chapter I examine the concept of decision making, first in relation to sensemaking theory. Decision making concerning risk can be adversely affected by failure to recognize and use available relevant data. Bazerman and Moore (2009) described this phenomenon as bounded awareness, and posited that it is caused by people's assumptions about where to focus their attention. Bounded awareness causes people to miss information due to focusing on another item, not recognizing that a situation has changed, or over-focusing on a specific event. Furthermore, research suggests people in group settings often discuss information that is already known by the group and do not consider unique or unshared information. In contrast, Weick, Sutcliffe, and Obstfeld (2005) said that managers often focus on obtaining scarce data instead of using data that is readily available to create action that fosters developing a better understanding of the situation. Consequently, prior to creating new processes for gathering data on risks, organizations can benefit from determining the existing data the institution already has available that may aid in the risk assessment process.

COSO's (2004) ERM framework is based on a rational decision-making model (further discussed below) that offers limited theoretical insight on how decisions actually occur in an organization. Sensemaking theory can offer more robust explanations of the factors associated with organizational decision-making than rational decision-making models. According to Smerek (2013), sensemaking focuses on action, shifting the analysis from individual events to a more comprehensive examination of the continuous stream of events and situations in organizational life. Weick (2007) further specifies that sensemaking is an ongoing and continuous process of change, enactment, selecting, and retention that people utilize to provide plausible meanings and to develop actions in response to a perceived abnormality or unexplained event. Weick et al. (2005) stated that once awareness of an abnormal event occurs, people start to assign new meaning to the previously unrecognized or undefined event. This leads to labeling and categorizing the event in order to provide stable interpretations that allow for the development of viable alternatives to manage and coordinate a response to the event.

Weick et al. (2005) state that sensemaking also entails building retrospective interpretations through a process of reciprocal exchanges between people and their environments. In this scenario, the actions of people iteratively interact with changes to the environment. The interactions between people and their environments continuously cycle to provide an ongoing retrospective update of the event. Consequently, certain interpretations of the event are selected and those determined plausible are retained by the individual and/or group as valid and meaningful.

Weick et al. (2005) pointed out that sensemaking is influenced by social factors and the sharing and coordination of information across the organization. The authors added that actions and discussions cycle back and forth during the sensemaking process as individuals use existing frameworks to help interpret events and, in some cases, develop new frameworks for interpretation. In essence, sensemaking is thus an ongoing dialogue people use to make sense of a situation in order to take action. Sensemaking is also driven by plausibility since people need accounts that are socially acceptable and credible in order to act, even if the account lacks accuracy (Weick, 1995). Social dimensions of sensemaking are consistent with Wall's (2011) finding that a person's perception of risk is related to the social context surrounding their assessment of the risk. Specific social dimensions Wall (2005) found central to how people understand risk include their experience, personal and group orientation, attachment to a place, and social class.

Beach and Connolly (2005) stated that image theory, similar to sensemaking theory, regards decision making as a social act in which groups and organizations influence and constrain individual decisions. More specifically, three types of images influence decision making: value images, trajectory images, and strategic images. Value images consist of the decision maker's values, morals, and ethics; and define standards for how things should be and how people ought to act in a given situation. Trajectory images address the decision maker's agenda, goals, and overall vision for the future. Strategic images speak to the individual's predictions of the future and plans for attaining their goals. Indeed, many complex organizations are comprised of people with diverse national and cultural backgrounds. Hence, the ERM risk assessment process needs to account for the diverse backgrounds, values, and beliefs of its members and the social dimensions of the decision-making processes that sensemaking and image theory illustrate.

Sensemaking theory also suggests that people do not rely solely on accurate information to act but instead base decisions on whether an action is plausible (Weick, 1995). Weick (1995) stated that executives' perceptions are often not accurate with regards to their organization and environment. Furthermore, most organizational action is time sensitive, and consequently a tradeoff exists between speed and accuracy. Therefore, sensemaking theory maintains that decisions on a course of action for an organization are often made based on plausibility, coherence, reasonableness, and explanations that are credible and socially acceptable. Consequently, ERM programs that overemphasize accuracy over plausibility may fail to address the practical and real ways people make decisions in today's complex organizational settings.

Chapter 9: Decision-Making II – Bias and Framing

Many things may influence decision making in a complex organization. In this chapter, I review two of these factors: bias and framing. Weick (1995) stated that sensemaking is "grounded in identity," as people make sense of events by questioning the effect it will have on who they are (p. 19). In other words, "Depending on who I am, my definition of what is 'out there' will also change" (Weick et al., 2005, p. 20). As such, human biases affect the quality of the risk decision-making process. Bazerman and Moore (2009) pointed out several common biases inherent to decision making, such as availability heuristics, representativeness heuristics, and confirmation heuristics. Availability heuristics biases are tendencies to judge events that are easily remembered or recalled as more common and likely to happen. Representative heuristics are biases caused by ignoring base rates and sample size, holding inaccurate beliefs that small samples of chance events will occur as a random data set, overestimating an abnormal event's effect on future outcomes, and overrating the probability of coincidental events. Confirmation heuristics biases include seeking information to confirm a person's beliefs, overvaluing initial assessments of an event, underestimating the probability of separate events, overconfidence in a person's judgment, and overestimating how accurately a person would have predicted an event that already occurred.

According to Weick (1995), there is a "fallacy of centrality" where people deny an event or situation exists simply because they do not know about it. This can cause people to avoid inquiring about a situation or event, or even to take a hostile position about its occurrence. In addition, Weick noted that outcomes can often precede a decision and create a situation where the focus of the decision maker is on justifying a course of action. This point was supported by McKenna (1999), who said that managers often make new decisions to validate previous decisions. Indeed, Weick (1995) cautioned that the retrospective nature of sensemaking can also lead to hindsight bias, where people reconstruct a negative event in a manner that draws incorrect conclusions about how previous actions and analyses contributed to the event. Moreover, such conclusions can result in unrealistic expectations that errors could have been corrected to prevent the event from occurring.

Biases can also be a byproduct of organizational factors. Argyris (1976) proposed that effective decision making can be impeded by ineffective work groups and organizational politics (e.g., coalition rivalries, failing to address organizational conflict, and avoiding uncertainty). In addition, individuals can impede decision making by competing excessively, focusing on personal gain, hoarding information, and improperly using power. Similarly, Bisel and Arterburn (2012) identified that employees may not provide negative feedback to their supervisors for a number of reasons, including: (a) being concerned over adverse repercussions, (b) believing supervisor will not listen, (c) doubting their expertise, and (d) viewing the supervisor as responsible for the issue. Furthermore, Williams et al. (2008) determined a manager's perception of risk is influenced by the amount of outcome uncertainty, whether losses are expected to be significant, whether options carry personal consequences, how the situation is framed, and the manager's desire to accept risk. The authors also concluded that the factors that indicate whether a manager will seek risk are limited to the potential for gain and how the situation is framed. Consequently, the ability of the ERM risk assessment process to overcome human bias in decision making is a critical consideration when designing processes to assess risk.

Decision-Making Framing

March and Shapira (1987) proposed that how a problem is framed can influence the perception of risk. Palazzo, Krings, and Hoffrage (2012) referred to rigid framing as a phenomenon that impairs a person's ability to see multiple options. The authors also said that consequences from past decisions frame the context for current decisions. Wood and Bandura (1989) pointed out the significance of the effect that situational demands and self-referent factors can have on the context of a decision. According to the authors, how people construe their cognitive ability, the controllability of the organization's performance, and the organization's complexity affect how people perceive the context surrounding a decision. Blaskovich and Taylor (2011) also found that decisions concerning risk are subject to framing problems. For example, the functional composition of groups assigned to identify and assess risk shapes how risk is prioritized in an organization. In addition, the authors stated that the existing tendency to rely heavily on accounting and finance functions for ERM has resulted in an overemphasis on financial risks. Arena et al. (2011) noted the importance of incorporating risk management specialists from different managerial levels into the ERM program so perspectives from different organizational levels are brought into the discussion on risk.

Effectively framing a problem can also enhance decision making. Stigliani and Ravasi (2012) pointed out that material representation, such as models and prototypes, can enhance the sensemaking and sensegiving processes. The authors continued to state that physical representations can increase cognitive capacity. Indeed, the authors argued that managers are well-served by complementing their analytical tools with material representations to stimulate new thinking. Similarly, Wood , Bostrom, Bridges, and Linkov (2012) proposed mapping out complex risks to identify knowledge gaps between a nonexpert's perception of risk and that of experts, in order to identify misconceptions nonexperts have about the risk. Such action can lead to focused educational programming that addresses mismatches or misunderstandings organizational members have about risk. Consequently, constructing material representations can be a powerful method for framing and facilitating discussions on risks.

Chapter 10: Decision Making and the COSO ERM Framework

As in the case of organizational change, with our new understanding of decision making, in this chapter I now connect the concept more directly to the ERM framework. The ERM decision-making conceptual area is composed of the following three elements of the COSO (2004) framework: event identification, risk assessment, and risk response. Research by Gates et al. (2012) showed that effective risk identification leads to better risk response, control, and monitoring of activities. In relation to ERM, Louisot and Ketcham (2009) proposed that ERM provides decision makers with a more complete picture of the organization's risks, which can improve the overall decision-making process of the organization. However, Paape and Speklé (2012) suggested that the COSO model is based on decision makers acting in a fully rational manner.

The COSO framework is similar to the rational decision-making model outlined by Bazerman and Moore (2009), which contains six steps (see Figure 4). The COSO event identification process first requires that organizations identify internal and external events that present risks or opportunities to the organization. The organization then assesses events to determine appropriate responses and control activities that ensure such responses are completed. The COSO framework labels this as event identification, while the rational decision-making process simply calls it "defining the problem." Next, each process proposes analyzing the problem or event, evaluating response options, and then selecting the most appropriate response. Consequently, the COSO decision-making process reflects a rational approach. Although the COSO framework also mentions identifying opportunities, little information on how this occurs as part of the ERM process or its relationship to risk is provided in the framework. Moreover, limited information is furnished on the actual processes complex organizations can utilize to evaluate the diverse set of risks the organization confronts.

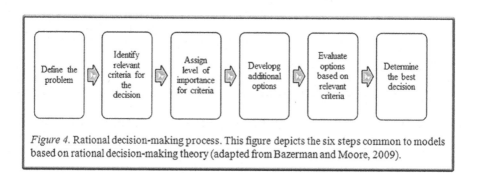

Figure 4. Rational decision-making process. This figure depicts the six steps common to models based on rational decision-making theory (adapted from Bazerman and Moore, 2009).

As Bazerman and Moore (2009) pointed out, rational decision-making models have considerable limits in real-world situations. The authors defined rational decision making as a process that results in the selection of the most logical option based on complete and accurate information and an accurate assessment of all the concerns of the decision maker(s). The authors cautioned that this is not how people normally make decisions. Weick et al. (2005) additionally posited that the large amount of ambiguous information, a wide range of problems, and time constraints restrict the application of rational decision-making models in organizational settings.

Sonenshein (2007) pointed out that people often do not engage in purposeful and comprehensive reasoning as rational decision-making theory proposes. In fact, people often use rational analysis *post hoc* to explain and justify their decisions. Sonenshein (2007) adds that people are reluctant to change their initial intuition and normally seek confirmatory evidence to justify their decisions. In addition, the author argued that people use rational analysis to explain retrospectively their decisions and actions in terms that justify their views and protect their self-identities. Furthermore, people need to be taught more elaborate cognitive processes to help overcome their natural tendency to respond to issues in automatic and habitual ways. Hence, ERM risk assessment processes need to be designed to overcome the limitations of rational decision-making processes and tendencies to seek information that confirms the correctness of a past decision.

The effectiveness the process an organization uses to evaluate risks is dependent on establishing clear risk tolerance levels and categories of risks. For example, Gates et al. (2012) found that an organization that clearly defines its risk tolerance levels and aligns their risk management goals with the organization's overall objectives is better at identifying risks. However, Blaskovich and Taylor (2011) cautioned that establishing an organizational risk appetite level is challenging. Moreover, the values, attitudes, and experiences of individuals, the organization's culture, and the focus of management can compromise establishing a risk appetite level. In addition, practitioners have noted dissatisfaction with the broadness of COSO's four risk categories (strategic, operations, reporting, and compliance) and the failure to define the activities covered by these categories. In particular, practitioners have noted concerns with the broadness of the operational category. Indeed, practitioners stated it was necessary for their organizations to define operational risk in a manner reflective of the risks common to the operations at their organization (Simkins, 2008). Consequently, establishing clear risk tolerance levels for the organization is beneficial, though organizations struggle with establishing these tolerance levels. This may be due to an overemphasis on using quantitative measures to assess risks and attempts to establish a universal risk tolerance level that applies across the full range of risks at an organization. For example, having a low tolerance level for risk may be appropriate when dealing with regulatory compliance issues; however, such restrictions may be counterproductive when looking at business risks, such as entry into a new market.

Chapter 11: Organizational Learning I – Learning Organizations

Moving to the third concept from management theory, in the remaining chapters in Part 2 I explain organizational learning, beginning with what constitutes a "learning organization." A learning organization is a place where people continually develop their ability to create the results they desire, where new and innovative methods of thinking are developed, and where people learn how to grow together (Senge, 1990, p. 3). Senge (1990) further explained that a learning organization is "an organization that is continually expanding its capacity to create its future" (p. 14). Popper and Lipshitz (2000) proposed that the feasibility of organizational learning is dependent on the level of uncertainty in the environment, the potential cost of errors, the level of professionalism, and leadership commitment to learning.

According to Argyris (1976), feedback and organizational learning are also important to effective decision making. Since decisions are often made based on incomplete information, it is critical that feedback be obtained to evaluate the effectiveness of the decision. Argyris (1976) further explained that the purpose of learning is to detect and correct errors due to lack of knowledge. Wood and Bandura (1989) stressed the importance of teaching people general rules and strategies for different situations and the need to provide opportunities to practice what is learned. The authors also pointed out the effect that situational demands and self-referent factors can have on decision making. Effective decision making is thus limited by breakdowns in organizational learning (Kim & Senge, 1994). According to Kim and Senge (1994), these breakdowns occur due to: (a) role constraints that prevent people from taking action, (b) individual actions that have unclear results for the organization, (c) fragmented learning that is limited to particular individuals or groups, and (d) unclear understanding of the impact of an action. As a result, people may misperceive the consequences of their actions, thus inhibiting their ability to learn from the situation.

Kim and Senge (1994) concluded that due to their focus on immediate organizational needs and problems, traditional training programs are often inadequate to create generative learning that develops new organizational capabilities. Instead, the authors suggested that organizations should create scenarios and learning experiences in which people can appreciate the long-term consequences of their decisions, have time to reflect on their habitual ways of thinking, and discover the systemic causes of problems. Schein (1993) also stated that attempts to create learning that leads to transformational change often fail since they lack depth. Indeed, to be effective, Schein (2010) posited that organizational learning requires significant commitment of an organization's energy and resources. Therefore, organizational learning, if used effectively, can play a key role in ERM implementation.

Overall, Stewart, Williams, Smith-Gratto, Black, and Kane (2011) found that pedagogies that focus on experiential learning and social interaction result in better organizational learning, as compared to technical-based pedagogies, due to their ability to develop shared mental models amongst organizational members. Indeed, technical-based pedagogies, such as lectures and case studies, rarely challenge how people think or their existing mental models. Furthermore, the authors proposed that improvements in organizational knowledge result in better decision making, and allow people to challenge their existing mental models. Senge (1990) also proposed that "mental models determine not only how we make sense of the world, but how we take action" (p. 164). He also suggested that existing mental models are the result of deeply ingrained assumptions, generalizations, and images of how people see the world. According to

Senge (1990), organizations can increase their capacity to challenge existing mental models by: (a) developing tools that promote personal understanding and reflection, (b) creating structures and processes that allow for the regularly application of mental models, and (c) fostering a culture that values open inquiry and questioning ideas and practices (p. 171). Therefore, an effective ERM program needs to address existing mental models and improve upon them to address organizational risk.

Chapter 12: Organizational Learning II – Sensemaking-Based and Team-Based Learning

There are several theories on how learning occurs within the organization. In this chapter, I review two of organizational learning theories and their applicability to ERM. Both theories illustrate that generating learning in organizations requires looking at learning as an ongoing process that requires multiple opportunities for people to absorb new knowledge.

Sensemaking-Based Learning

Kim and Senge (1994) presented learning as a cycle composed of observation, assessment, design, and implementation (OADI). The OADI cycle seeks to foster learning that generates new mental models and increases organizational capabilities. The OADI cycle is very similar to the COSO framework's model of event identification (observation), risk assessment (assessment), risk response (design), and control and monitoring activities (implementation); and also reflects elements of the sensemaking process. Brock et al. (2008)

found that a sensemaking-based curriculum can shift an individual's mental models and is particularly useful in helping people deal with complex and ambiguous situations. Sensemaking can also help people understand and overcome personal biases that are common to decision making. Brock et al.'s (2008) model focuses on five sensemaking processes: framing, affect, forecasting, self-reflection, and information integration. Items covered in the framing process include problem appraisal, goal assessment, framing, monitoring, and perceived threats or opportunities. The affect process involves emotion regulation. The forecasting process includes autobiographical extraction, solution revision, and contingency planning. The self-reflection process includes self-based and other-based perceptions. Last, the information integration process involves solution appraisal and the advantages and disadvantages each course of action has for impacted stakeholders. Hence, sensemaking based learning may be an effect at developing the people's abilities to evaluate complex and ambiguous risks. For example, risks associated with new strategic initiatives at an organization are often hard to identify and evaluate. Thus, sensemaking-based training could help organizational leaders learn how to evaluate risks that are difficult to recognize and with which the institution lacks experience managing.

Maitlis (2005) used sensemaking theory to explain the process people go through to understand organizational reality, identifying four forms of organizational sensemaking: guided, fragmented, restricted, and minimal. The author based the model on two critical types of sensemaking roles: (a) the leader as sensegiving (level of control), and (b) the stakeholder as sensegiving (level of animation). In this context, the author defined sensegiving as "the process of attempting to influence the sensemaking and meaning construction of others toward a preferred redefinition of organizational reality" (p. 22). Maitlis (2005) proposed that guided organizational sensemaking produces the most robust form of organizational sensemaking. In this scenario, leader sensegiving is highly controlled and involves such activities as scheduled meetings, formal committees, and planned events with restricted attendance. Guided sensemaking also entails stakeholders that use high-animated sensegiving processes involving the robust flow of information. Maitlis (2005) found behavior common to this type of sensegiving includes stakeholders that actively engage in shaping interpretations of events and intense reporting between leadership and the board, executive teams, and other stakeholders. Complex organizations can foster ERM implementation by having leaders and stakeholders engage in sensegiving activities. For example, Kezar (2014) suggested that sensegiving vehicles commonly used at an organization should include extensive and ongoing conversational, collaborative, and cross-functional teams, public events and presentations, open discussions about challenges faced by the organization, and opportunities to contribute to the vision and direction of the organization. Consequently, building these sensegiving vehicles into the ERM program can foster organizational learning on risk management practices while also serving to embed these concepts into the process and culture at the institution.

Thomas, Sussman, and Henderson (2001) investigated how sensemaking theory explains the means by which an organization creates strategic learning. According to the authors, the goal of strategic learning is to focus attention on events that directly supports an organization's business strategy. The authors highlighted four dimensions of this process: defining the event set, data acquisition, interpretation, and packaging. Selection of event sets focuses on the ability to explore organizational problems and test strategic beliefs. Data acquisition involves a purposeful collection of real-time data

89

relevant to the event from across the organization. The authors suggested using a template to guide the collection of data. Subject experts then engage in extensive dialogue on the data in order to generate multiple interpretations of the event applicable to current and future contexts. Lesson learned are packaged for distribution across the organization. The authors stressed the knowledge developed in the process needs to be of high quality so consumers of the information value and willingly use the knowledge. The authors found that this type of learning generates useful knowledge that is dispersed across the organization, that learning is a critical and entwined part of sensemaking, and learning uses sensemaking mechanisms and validated processes. Although this level of effort may not be applicable to routine organizational risks, such an effort may be of value when assessing risks associated with critical strategic decisions at complex organizations.

Mumford, Connelly, and Brown (2008) proposed that sensemaking is critical to ethical decision-making processes in three areas: (a) the need to realize a situation has ethical implications, (b) the lack of simple yes/no answers, and (c) the implications sensemaking and mental models have for forecasting the outcomes of decisions. To test these propositions, the authors conducted research using a

90

sensemaking-based training model. They found that sensemaking-based training improves ethical decision-making capabilities due to the training's ability to provide context for the application of rules and guidance, generate new mental models that are applicable to situations with ethical implications, and acknowledge real-life complexity and ambiguity in the decision-making process. Ethical decisions share similar complexity as decisions on risks that are both hard to identify and lack quantifiable measures or other simpler decision-making criteria. Consequently, training on assessment methods for complex risks may benefit from the application of the sensemaking-based training approach offered by Mumford et al. Therefore, the literature suggests sensemaking-based methodologies can be effective for training people to evaluate risks.

Team-Based Learning

Senge (1990) argued that thought is mainly a collective experience. According to Senge (1990), teams make or implement most of today's important decisions, however teams often fail to realize their potential due to a tendency to focus on discussion where one person's view prevails over another. To counter this tendency, Senge (1990) proposed that teams should learn how to foster dialogue that allows the group to explore complex and difficult issues. Three conditions are required to develop this dialogue: (a) suspending assumptions, (b) viewing other team members as colleagues, and (c) utilizing a facilitator to keep the team on track. Senge acknowledged that it is challenging for people to suspend their beliefs, and teams may encounter defensive routines. However, teams that are truly committed to learning can overcome defensive behavior.

Higgins, Weiner, and Young (2012) found that team-based learning can be improved by ensuring that teams are composed of people with positional diversity. According to the authors, conditions that enable team-based learning include: understanding team membership requirements, stable membership, work that requires interdependence, a clear purpose, norms of conduct, supportive reward systems, and members that could also serve as mentors. Higgins et al. (2012) also found that teams with good positional diversity are able to reduce the adverse effects of having poor enabling conditions. Team-based learning should be part of the ERM program due to the social nature within which risks are understood in an organization and the collective nature of program implementation at complex organizations.

92

Chapter 13: Organizational Learning III

– Action and Absorptive Capacity

The theories of action and absorptive capacity, the focus of this chapter, can be used to analyze how organizational learning influences ERM implementation. Senge (1990) stated that a learning organization is a place where people continually develop their ability to create the results they desire, where new and innovative methods of thinking are developed, and where people learn how to grow together. Argyris (1976) proposed two types of organizational learning in his theories of action. First, single-loop learning is characterized by people using strategies "to control the relevant environment and tasks unilaterally and to protect themselves and their group unilaterally" (p. 368). This type of learning is characterized by controlling behavioral strategies, such as defensiveness, closedness, lack of sharing information, and limited decision-making capabilities. In contrast, double-learning is "governed by valid information, free and informed choice, and internal commitment" (p. 369). Double-looped learning is characterized by sharing information with relevant decision makers, use of valid information, and a willingness to discuss and challenge ideas. Consequently, theories of action are useful to analyze how organizational learning influences and can enhance ERM implementation.

Absorptive capacity is defined as the collective ability of an organization to recognize the value of new information and utilize it for business purposes (Sun & Anderson, 2010). Absorptive capacity is characterized by an organization's ability to recognize the value of information, assimilate information, and apply information. Absorptive capacity is comprised of four capabilities: (a) acquisition, which is an organization's ability to identify and acquire external knowledge; (b) assimilation, which is the processes the organization uses to understand external knowledge; (c) transformation, which entails how the organization combines the new knowledge with existing knowledge; and (d) exploration, which is an organization's ability to use the new knowledge for competitive advantage (Sun & Anderson, 2010). As such, absorptive capacity is useful to analyze how organizations can acquire and utilize external knowledge as part of the ERM implementation process.

In sum, the literature indicates organizations implementing ERM need to develop learning strategies that expand people's capabilities and mental models for assessing and managing risks. However, changing mental models is a deep, complex learning process (Kim & Senge, 1994). As such, this level of learning requires that complex organizations utilize more comprehensive and effective methodologies than those found in traditional training approaches. Moreover, organizational learning must provide people with the cognitive ability to assess and respond to the complexity and uncertainty inherent in decisions on risk. Consequently, organizations must acknowledge the importance of organizational learning in the ERM implementation process and using educational programs based on sensemaking-based and team-based learning models.

Chapter 14: Organizational Learning and COSO's ERM Framework

In the final chapter of Part 2, I link organizational learning to the following components of the COSO (2004) framework for ERM implementation: information and communication and monitoring. According to COSO (2004), organizations must identify and capture critical information on ERM and communicate it to employees in a manner that allows them to make informed decisions. Additionally, top management must communicate a clear message on ERM responsibilities across the organization. This relates to Schein's (2010) proposition that effective and meaningful communication of information across the organization is central to building a learning culture. However, COSO's focus is on ERM information management systems and processes, not on how an organization can create an environment conducive to learning and problem solving. Additionally, COSO stated that a key challenge with information management is collating large volumes of data into actionable information. Indeed, Senge (1990) said that today's environment creates far more information than people can absorb or manage, and that this information overload adds to the complexity organizations face.

Weick (1995) argued that organizations often mistakenly think they need more information when instead they need better values, priorities, and clarity so they can effectively determine what is important to the organization. Consequently, complex organizations need to develop communications strategies in conjunction with their learning programs to enhance people's ability to make informed decisions on risk.

There are two types of monitoring activities for ERM implementation: ongoing activities that build monitoring into the day-to-day activities, and separate evaluations conducted by either internal staff or by external parties (COSO, 2004). Concerning the monitoring component, Schein (2010) pointed out the importance of creating agreement in the organization on what and how activities are measured. According to Schein (2010), this is a particular concern when organizational subcultures have different concepts on what and how to evaluate results. In addition, an organization must agree on how to communicate monitoring information and on who is responsible for taking action on that information. Hence, complex organizations need to come to agreement on how the institution will monitor its risks and what measures will be taken to control risks.

Part 3: Factors Affecting ERM Adoption and Implementation

Moving to the application of the theories discussed in Part 2, in Part 3 I examine the range of factors that can affect ERM adoption and implementation. More specifically, I first explain the process organizations experience when implementing a significant initiative such as ERM. I then review the scholarly research on why organizations adopt an ERM strategy and the critical success factors that enable the successful implementation of ERM. In the final chapter of Part 3, I synthesize the findings of the literature, suggesting an evidence-based model for ERM implementation.

Chapter 15: The Program Implementation Process

In order to examine the factors affecting ERM adoption and implementation, it is essential to have a thorough understanding of the process itself. The findings from Leseure, Bauer, Birdi, Neely, and Denyer's (2004) systematic review on the process organizations use to identify and implement external business practices provide a framework for conceptualizing ERM implementation. They use the phrase "adopting promising practices" to denote the externally-developed management practices an organization decides to implement. Examples include total quality management, just-in-time practices, and business process re-engineering. As a management practice broadly affecting the organization, ERM is similar to the examples of promising practices provided by the authors. As illustrated in Figure 5, the implementation process involves five stages: (a) the adoption decision, (b) set-up (adaption), (c) implementation, (d) ramp-up, and (e) integration.

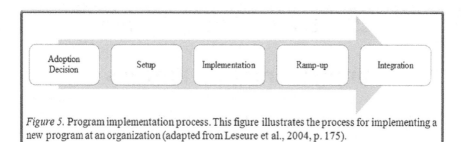

Figure 5. Program implementation process. This figure illustrates the process for implementing a new program at an organization (adapted from Leseure et al., 2004, p. 175).

The adoption phase encompasses all events that lead to the decision to adopt a business practice. The set-up (adaption) is the stage in which the decision to proceed is made, and the approach to implementing the new practice is customized to meet the organizational context. Leseure et al. (2004) found that practices "pushed" on an organization by regulations, management, or external norms and that did not meet a perceived need seldom resulted in performance improvements. In addition, the authors suggested that to be successful, practices must be adapted to the organizational context and resource needs must be developed at the set-up stage.

Continuing along the process, the implementation phase is the launch of the program. The focus at this stage is activities that have short-term horizons for completion. Leseure et al. (2004) stated that factors critical at this stage include a project champion, a well-designed program,

100

training, supervisor reinforcement, and a developing commitment to the program. Next, the organization starts to use the promising practice during the ramp-up stage. At this stage, it is important that the practice is tailored to meet the needs of individual employees or groups versus a generic one-size-fits-all approach. This requires flexible approaches and communicating the practice to all levels in the organization. Lastly, the integration stage occurs after positive results have been achieved from implementing the practice. Gradually, the new practice becomes a part of the routine operations of the organization. Leseure et al. (2004) found that integrating new practices requires persistence in order to embed the practice into the organization's accepted knowledge base.

Complex organizations considering ERM will likely go through a similar process of identifying ERM as a new business practice to adopt at the institution. If this decision is favorable, the organization will then go through the process of designing the ERM program, introducing and utilizing ERM, and integrating ERM so that it becomes an accepted practice at the organization.

Chapter 16: Why Organizations Adopt an ERM Strategy

In this chapter, I outline the logic behind why organizations adopt an ERM strategy to manage their risks. The findings are based on a comprehensive review of scholarly research on ERM. Here, I explain what the desired outcomes are that organizations seek to address by adopting ERM. The discussion starts with an overview of studies that focus on the financial value of adopting ERM and whether ERM increases a firm's value. The conversation then shifts to performance outcomes that drive organizations to adopt ERM such as: (a) enhanced regulatory compliance; (b) increased accountability; (c) improved performance and decision making; (d) pressure from board members, senior leadership, and external stakeholders; (e) enhanced understanding of organizational risk; and (f) improved ability to navigate crises. I conclude with an overview of how an organization's rationale for implementing ERM can influence the type of ERM program it implements.

Financial Value

Initial studies on ERM focused on whether ERM is associated with increased firm value.

Hence, it is prudent to begin by reviewing the empirical research on ERM and increased financial performance. Studies in this section largely used regression modeling with publicly available data on organizations and their financial filings to ascertain whether there is a correlation between ERM and profitability.

Liebenberg and Hoyt's (2003) study of 26 U.S.-based firms from the financial and industrial sectors and one airline company found a positive and significant correlation between higher leveraged firms, firms with more external funding, and the appointment of a chief risk officer (CRO). The authors argued that firms that appointed a CRO were more likely to engage in ERM, and that employing a CRO helped to alleviate lender concerns over agency costs. Ultimately, the authors suggested that firms that appoint a CRO are likely to see increased value due to better coordinated risk management and an increased ability to communicate the organization's risk profile to stakeholders. A subsequent study by Hoyt and Liebenberg (2011) with a larger sample population, which consisted of 117 U.S. insurance firms, found organizations that implemented ERM were larger, less leveraged, less opaque (easier for outside firms to evaluate), and had less financial slack (more access to liquid funds) and lower return volatility. Moreover, the

103

results of this study suggested that insurers that engaged in ERM had value levels approximately 20% higher than those that did not engage in ERM. However, the direction of this correlation was not clear, and did not indicate if ERM led to the improvements in these variables, or whether firms with these characteristics were more likely to implement ERM.

In another study, Eckles, Hoyt, and Miller (2014) analyzed 69 U.S.-based insurance firms, and found that organizations that adopt ERM see greater reductions in risk per dollar spent on risk. However, the authors cautioned that these benefits are gradual at first but become stronger over time. Similarly, Farrell and Gallagher's (2015) research suggested that the financial benefits of ERM increase as the ERM program matures and integrates with the strategic and routines practices of an organization. Grace, Leverty, Phillips, and Shimpi's (2015) study of the insurance sector suggested ERM contributes to increased firm value. This is particularly salient in organizations with a dedicated risk management function and a risk manager that reports to the CEO. Last, Aabo, Fraser, and Simkins's (2005) case study of a Canadian utility company found that ERM had a positive influence on credit ratings, which resulted in substantial annual savings on the interest paid on debt.

Conversely, McShane et al. (2011) surveyed 82 U.S.-based publicly traded insurers and found a correlation between increased levels of traditional risk management practices and firm value, but not between ERM and firm value. Likewise, Lin, Wen, and Yu's (2012) analysis of 85 publicly traded U.S.-based property and casualty insurers from 2000 to 2007 found ERM to have a negative effect on firm value when controlling for independent risk management practices. Moreover, Beasley, Pagach, and Warr's (2008) analysis of 120 U.S.-based publicly traded firms did not support broad statements about shareholder benefits or reduced costs for firms that adopted ERM. However, the latter study suggested shareholders of large firms with limited cash supplies value ERM. Last, a study by Onder and Ergin (2012) of 50 financial companies listed on the Istanbul Stock Exchange found higher levels of ERM implementation correlated with highly leveraged and, to a lesser extent, larger firms. However, they did not find a correlation between profitability and ERM implementation.

As such, the evidence on whether ERM increases firm value is mixed. Six studies found a correlation between ERM and improved financial performance, and one indicated that stakeholders valued ERM in large organizations with limited access to capital (Beasley et al., 2008;

Eckles et al., 2014; Hoyt & Liebenberg, 2011; Liebenberg & Hoyt, 2003). However, it is unclear if ERM is the actual mechanism that leads to improved performance or whether improved financial performance is caused by other factors, such as better management practices or simply the perception that the firm is taking measures to address risk. Conversely, one study found a correlation between increased traditional risk management practices (McShane et al., 2011), and another found lower value associated with ERM when controlling for independent risk management practices (Lin et al., 2012).

Studies in this area used rather abstract methodologies (e.g., regression modeling) to analyze publicly available financial data in order to identify correlations between ERM and firm value. Only one study assessed the effect the maturity of an ERM program has on financial performance (Farrell & Gallagher, 2015), while other studies only used a CRO as a proxy for ERM. Therefore, although it may be logical to argue that organizations that are more competent at managing risks will see improved financial performance, the research to date provides limited and inconclusive evidence to support organizations adopting ERM purely from an increased financial value perspective. Table 1 provides a summary of the findings on ERM and firm value.

Additional Factors

The literature showed organizations adopt ERM for reasons other than to increase financial value. For example, Arena et al.'s (2011) multiple case study of nine Italian nonfinancial companies indicated that the three main reasons firms adopted ERM were corporate governance, internal auditing, and decision making. The authors found that corporate implementation of ERM related to the need to comply with governance codes and regulations and board of directors' reporting requirements. Alternatively, internal auditing groups used ERM to compare their analysis of risk with those of local managers, to plan future audits, and for inclusion in audit reports. The authors also found ERM supported operational decision making at all nine companies; however, only three organizations used ERM for corporate-wide decision making. Similarly, Hayne and Free's (2014) research suggested that the three reasons organizations adopted ERM were due to new regulations, the desire to self-insure, and requirements that risk be auditable.

Table 1

Enterprise Risk Management and Financial Value

Outcome	Authors	Mechanism(s)	Context
Positive financial value	Aabo et al. (2005)	Improved credit rating resulted in savings due to reduced interest rates on loans	Canadian utility company
	Eckles et al. (2014)	Firms that adopted ERM saw greater reductions in risk per dollar spent on risk.	U.S.-based insurance firms
	Hoyt & Liebenberg (2011)	Insurers that engaged in ERM had value levels approximately 20% higher than those that did not engage in ERM.	U.S.-based insurance firms
	Liebenberg & Hoyt (2003)	Higher leveraged firms were more likely to appoint a CRO and adopt ERM to reduce lender agency cost concerns, which led to higher firm value.	U.S. firms from the financial services, industrial sector, and airline industry
	Grace et al. (2015)	Firms with ERM programs, a dedicated risk management function, and a risk manager that reports to the CEO show increased cost and revenue efficiency	U.S.-based insurance firms
	Farrell & Gallagher (2015)	Financial benefits of ERM increase with ERM program maturity	North America, UK, and Australia firms from a wide range of industries
Negative financial value	Lin et al. (2012)	When controlling for independent risk management practices, ERM was found to have a negative effect on firm value.	Publicly traded U.S.-based property and casualty insurers

	McShane et al. (2011)	A correlation was found between increased levels of traditional risk management and firm value, but not between ERM and firm value.	United States-based publicly traded insurers
	Onder & Ergin (2012)	No correlation was found between higher profit levels and ERM implementation, but a correlation was found between highly leverage and larger firms and ERM implementation.	Financial firms listed on the Istanbul Stock Exchange
Uncertain financial value	Beasley et al. (2008)	No support was found for broad statements about shareholders benefits or costs for firms adopting ERM; however, the study suggested shareholders of large firms with limited cash supplies value ERM.	U.S.-based publicly traded firms

Hallowell, Molenaar, and Fortunato (2013) suggested that experienced executives and senior leaders at the U.S. Department of Transportation perceived that ERM offered the following benefits: (a) better use of data for decision making, (b) improved consideration of political factors and stakeholder expectations, (c) enhanced performance and strategic planning, (d) better contingency planning, and (e) an improved risk management culture. Similarly, in Arnold et al.'s (2011) survey of 113 North American chief audit executives, the authors concluded that a strong ERM program in conjunction with flexible organizational structures enhances an organization's ability to respond to new

109

regulatory requirements. Arnold et al.'s (2012) subsequent study of ERM at transnational supply chain companies found that ERM promotes absorptive capacity and reduces overall global risk and business-to-business e-commerce risk. Fraser et al. (2008) noted that executives charged with ERM stated that the top reason for adopting ERM was to improve organizational understanding of managing risk. Additional reasons cited by executives for adopting ERM included improved governance, better allocation of resources, enhanced decision making, and minimizing surprises to the organization. Similarly, Gates's (2006) survey of 271 respondents from multiple industry sectors located in North America, Continental Europe, and the United Kingdom found the top five drivers for adopting ERM were: (a) corporate governance requirements, (b) better understanding of strategic and operational risks, (c) regulatory pressures, (d) board requests, and (e) development of a competitive advantage. Gates et al. (2012) further found that ERM created greater management consensus, improved decision making, and increased accountability. Last, a survey of Chinese construction firms by Zhao, Hwang, and Low (2015) found motives for adopting ERM include improving decision making, reduce costs, losses and earning volatility, gain competitive advantage, and improve control   of larger projects.

110

Seik, Yu, and Li (2011), in a study on U.S. publicly-traded property and casualty insurance companies, found those with strong ERM programs were more capable of navigating the 2008 financial crisis. In addition, the authors suggested that firms with poor ERM programs performed worse during the crisis than the firms without ERM programs. However, due to the small sample size of their study, caution needs to be exercised when drawing strong inferences from their findings. Aabo et al. (2005) noted that one company viewed adopting ERM as a means to protect its reputation, while Arena, Arnaboldi, and Azzone (2010) noted ERM implementation was driven at one organization by a recent organizational crisis that damaged the company's image with stakeholders. The authors further found that the company that implemented ERM in response to a recent crisis had more success with ERM implementation than did those that adopted ERM to address compliance and corporate governance concerns. Di Serio et al. (2011) found the benefits realized from adopting ERM included buildup of shareholder trust, prevention of interruptions to operations, perceived increase in operation results, and enhanced identification of opportunities and threats.

In Huber and Rothstein's (2013) case study of risk management at a U.K.

university system, the authors noted that the need for more integrated approaches to risk management was driven by three factors. First, organizational complexity in the university system had spurned a wide variety of methods for managing adverse outcomes, which sometimes contradicted each other. Second, government pressure necessitated that the university system adopt practices from the business sector in order to provide rational and legitimacy for decisions on risks. Third, the system was required to meet social and political demands for accountability. In addition, the authors noted that academic risks were increasingly framed as reputational risks.

This set of studies suggests that desires to improve corporate governance, compliance, and decision-making processes influence the decision to adopt ERM. In addition, aspirations to improve risk management and crisis management capabilities, to meet regulatory and stakeholder expectations, and to create a competitive advantage influence the decision to adopt ERM. Last, organizations also appear to adopt ERM to protect their reputation and to demonstrate they have processes in place to manage risks. Consequently, there are multiple reasons an organization may decide to adopt ERM beyond those that are purely profit driven. Indeed, these factors may be antecedents to the realization of improved financial performance. That is, organizations that are successful at using ERM to improve governance, compliance, decision-making process, and to protect their reputation and meet stakeholder expectations will, in turn, realize improved financial performance.

Characteristics of Organizations That Adopt ERM

In survey by Beasley et al. (2005) of 123 chief auditors from multiple industries, such as banking, education, and insurance, the authors found that firms with more robust ERM programs were positively correlated with: (a) the presence of a chief risk officer, (b) an independent board of directors, (c) explicit requests from the chief executive or financial officer, (d) larger firms, and (e) firms audited by the big four. Interestingly, the authors found that U.S. firms had less advanced ERM programs. Additionally, di Serio, de Oliveira, and Schuch (2011), through case studies of three Brazilian firms, found ERM implementation was simply driven by demands from upper management.

Kleffner et al. (2003)'s study of 118 Canadian organizations from the energy, manufacturing, transportation, finance, government, nonprofit, and other sectors showed that firms adopted ERM due to influence from risk managers, pressure from boards of directors, and the need to comply with industry guidelines. In addition, the authors suggested that firms from the energy sector, organizations where the risk manager reports to the vice president of finance, and those that rely more heavily on external resources were more likely to adopt ERM. The authors noted that firms who recently adopted ERM tended to exhibit such behaviors as: (a) increased public disclosures via the Intranet, (b) development of company-wide risk management policies, (c) increased board interaction, (d) higher external board membership, (e) heightened awareness of operational risk, (f) more frequent reports on risk management to leadership and the board, and (g) increased levels of shared decision making across departments. The authors also found that firms with existing separate risk management functions were less likely to adopt ERM.

Consistent with other studies, Lundqvist's (2015) survey of publicly traded Nordic companies showed that larger-sized firms adopt ERM to provide a governance structure to manage that increase in agency problems associated with larger organizations. Additionally, Lundqvist (2015) suggested that firms with a CEO on the board of directors are less likely to adopt ERM. Lundqvist suggested that CEOs are reluctant to accept an additional governance structure such as

114

ERM, and as board members, are able to discourage the board from requiring that the organization adopt ERM. Daud, Haron, and Ibrahim (2011) conducted a study of publicly traded Malaysian companies from multiple nonfinancial industries to determine whether the quality of an organization's board of directors influences ERM implementation. This was assessed in three areas: board structure, composition, and meetings. The authors found a correlation between a higher quality board of directors and ERM implementation, and asserted that this was due to board members' desires to protect their reputation. However, one factor potentially affecting the findings of this study is that data was collected via a survey sent to chief executives and board members, and thus the quality of the board was determined by members' self-reporting on the performance of boards of which they were members, thus potentially biasing the findings.

Pagach and Warr (2011) conducted an analysis of U.S.-based public organizations that had announced the appointment of a senior risk officer between 1992 and 2005. The authors suggested that larger firms with riskier stock returns and higher levels of cash flow volatility were more likely to appoint a chief risk officer. They argued that the appointment of a chief risk officer was a proxy for indicating that an organization

115

adopted ERM. The authors also found that organizations that had CEOs with risk-taking incentives were more likely to adopt ERM. Similarly, Paape and Speklé (2012) found that large, publicly traded, and/or financial organizations tend to have more advanced ERM programs. Additionally, Kanhai, Ganesh, and Muhwandavaka (2014) found that the primary reason banks in Zimbabwe adopted ERM was to develop a portfolio view of enterprise risks.

Findings from this set of studies suggest that the characteristics of an organization influence whether it will decide to adopt ERM. Hence, larger organizations operating in high risk or highly regulated environments are more likely to adopt ERM. Organizations with leadership that actively seek information on the risks the organization faces and who desire to improve risk management are more likely to adopt ERM. Although one study suggested that leadership may avoid adopting ERM if it is perceived as an additional management burden (Lundqvist, 2015). Last, having an existing senior level person responsible for risk management also appears to increase the chances an organization will adopt ERM. This evidence suggests that ERM will be more attractive to larger organizations with operations that present higher levels of risks. Examples of such operations may include global operations, biomedical research, and the

116

use of private organizations to commercialize university-developed innovations. Such operations expose the institution to higher levels of risk and increased regularity requirements. Moreover, organizations with leadership and a board of directors that views effective risk management as critical to the success of the institution are more likely to adopt ERM.

The Adoption Decision's Influence on the Type of ERM Program

Two studies in the dataset suggested that the reasons an organization adopts ERM influence the type of ERM program an organization implements. First, in a case study of two large U.S. banks, Mikes (2009) found one institution adopted ERM to address a strong concern for shareholder value. This led to an ERM program that focused on risk quantification and a lack of discussion on nonquantifiable strategic risks. The second institution looked at risk management from a corporate governance perspective, which resulted in a more holistic approach to risk management that focused on both quantitative and qualitative approaches, and an emphasis on strategic decision making.

Second, Arena et al.'s (2010) 7-year longitudinal case study of three Italian firms identified three rationalities for risk management: (a) compliance, (b) improved corporate governance, and (c) enhanced performance. Firms that only focused on compliance failed to motivate managers to increase their knowledge of risk, and organizations that framed ERM as a corporate governance initiative limited ERM to an internal control process. However, organizations that proposed ERM as a means to improve performance were able to install accountability for risk throughout the organization and motivate managers to envision both potential risks and opportunities. The authors found implementation of ERM challenged an organization's existing risk management practices, and that whether ERM caused a shift in the decision-making mindset of managers was contingent on whether risk was perceived as a real problem. Moreover, ERM change agents significantly influenced how ERM was implemented but were also constrained by the existing organization. The authors also suggested that ERM was only perceived as a real problem if it was framed in operational terms and linked to performance, or if a recent adverse event had influenced how the organization conceived uncertainty. These studies suggest that organizations that adopt ERM to improve organizational governance and performance are more likely to have ERM programs that positively affect the organization's risk management practices.

In sum, there is a diverse body of evidence from a wide range of business sectors that suggests organizations adopt ERM for the following reasons: (a) compliance, (b) increased understanding of organizational risks, (c) improved decision-making and performance, (d) internal pressures, (e) external stakeholder demands, and (f) corporate governance. These factors, combined with normative forces for increased accountability and risk management, are also powerful drivers for organizations to adopt ERM. Tables 2 and 3 provide a summary of the compliance and performance outcomes organizations hope to achieve by adopting ERM.

Table 2

Compliance Outcomes Organizations Desire from Adopting an ERM

Strategy

Desired Outcome	Number of studies	Authors
Regulatory compliance	6	Arena et al. (2010); Arnold et al. (2011); Hayne & Free (2014); Huber & Rothstein (2013); Kallenberg (2009); Kleffner et al. (2003)
Governance	6	Arena et al. (2010, 2011); Fraser et al. (2008); Gates (2006); Lundqvist (2015); Mikes (2009); Muralidhar (2010)
Stakeholder expectations	4	Di Serio et al. (2011); Hallowell et al. (2013); Kallenberg (2009); Mikes (2009);
Board of director/senior leadership demands	4	Di Serio et al. (2011); Gates (2006); Kleffner et al. (2003); Muralidhar (2010)
Auditability	2	Arena et al. (2011); Gates (2206); Hayne & Free (2014)
Accountability	2	Gates et al. (2012); Huber & Rothstein (2013)

Table 3

Performance Outcomes Organizations Desire from Adopting an ERM

Strategy

Desired Outcome	Number of studies	Authors
Risk management (culture, understanding risk, reducing risk)	6	Arnold et al. (2012); Clyde-Smith (2014); Fraser et al. (2008); Gates (2006); Hallowell et al. (2013); Kanhai et al. (2014)
Decision making	5	Arena et al. (2011); Fraser et al. (2008); Gates et al. (2012); Hallowell et al. (2013); Zhao et al. (2015)
Performance (general)	4	Arena et al. (2010); Di Serio et al. (2011); Hallowell et al. (2013); Muralidhar (2010)
Crises/contingency planning and response	3	Fraser et al. (2008); Hallowell et al. (2013); Seik et al. (2011)
Response to new regulations	1	Arnold et al. (2011)
Absorptive capacity	1	Arnold et al. (2012)
Resource allocation	1	Fraser et al. (2008)
Competitive advantage	1	Gates (2006); Zhao et al. (2015)
Management consensus	1	Gates et al. (2012)
Improved strategic planning	1	Hallowell et al. (2013)
Organizational complexity	1	Huber & Rothstein (2013)
Reduce costs/earning volatility	1	Zhao et al. (2015)

Chapter 17: Factors Influencing the Implementation of an ERM Program

In this chapter, I now turn to the factors that increase the likelihood an organization will be successful when implementing an ERM strategy. More specifically, I provide an overview of the findings from a comprehensive review of scholarly research on the factors that are both critical to and inhibit successful ERM implementation, namely: (a) management practices, (b) culture, (c) change agents, (d) program design, (e) implementation barriers, (f) decision making, and (g) organizational learning.

Management Practices

Lundqvist's (2014) study of 153 firms from Scandinavian countries (i.e., Sweden, Norway, Finland, and Denmark) identified four pillars for ERM implementation. The first two are not unique to ERM and can be considered antecedents to its implementation. They include factors related to general business processes associated with the organization's internal environment (e.g., training, codes of conduct, performance measures, defined responsibilities, and business strategies) and control activities (e.g., policies, procedures, and methods to report suspect behavior). The third pillar is generic to managing risks for different types of events that influence the organization from financial, compliance, reputational, and strategic perspectives. However, activities in this area do not differentiate between silo-based or integrated risk management approaches. The last pillar is reflective of ERM and speaks to managing risk in a holistic manner with clearly defined risk management tolerances and responsibilities that include senior leadership and board oversight and accountability. The last pillar highlights that ERM provides a governance structure for how an organization manages the processes it uses to understand and control risks. Hence, the study showed that ERM provides that overall framework for how an organization executes the activities outlined in the first three pillars.

Gates et al. (2012) developed a survey based on the eight components of the COSO framework (i.e., internal environment, objective setting, event identification, risk assessment, risk response, control activities, information and communication, and monitoring) and sent it to 150 audit and risk management executives in various industries and countries. The results supported the COSO framework's ability to lead to better ERM implementation. Moreover, the findings showed that ERM enhances management and improves business performance. However, Arena et al. (2010) found that strict adherence to the COSO framework resulted in the program being perceived as solely focused on compliance and limited acceptance by managers with oversight of key risks.

Similarly, Zhao, Hwang, and Low's (2013) study of Chinese construction firms found that the top five critical success factors for ERM implementation, from highest to lowest, were: (a) senior leadership commitment; (b) risk identification, analysis, and response; (c) clear objectives at each organizational level; (d) a designated "owner" of the ERM program; and (e) integration of ERM into routine business processes. Zhao, Hwang, and Low's (2014a) survey of 35 Chinese construction firms asked respondents to rate their organization's ERM implementation level based on 66 ERM best practices identified in a previous study. Respondents rated risk communication, objective settings, risk-aware culture, risk identification, analysis, and response, and leveraging risk as opportunity as the top five items firms implement as part of their ERM programs. As a follow-up the survey, Zhao, Hwang, and Low (2014b) conducted case studies on three firms from the initial survey population (one from each firm size: large, mid, and small) to confirm or disconfirm survey findings. The authors found support for the initial findings; however, firm size significantly influenced the extent to which ERM was implemented at the firms. In addition, Liu, Zou, and Gong's (2013) case study of two international Chinese construction firms found that ERM improves operational risk management practices.

Research by Clyde-Smith (2014) on the implementation of ERM at a new multipartner research institution showed that the working group charged with developing an ERM program felt ERM needed to be consistent with existing policies, and that risk management processes requires coordination at high levels while deferring the management of specific risks to individual stakeholders. Hallowell et al. (2013) found that effectively implementing ERM requires: (a) integrating ERM into all organizational functions, (b) developing a clear organization-wide understanding of ERM, (c) involving employees in the development of the ERM program, and (d) forming a small-dedicated implementation team and providing that team with adequate resources. Furthermore, Gordon, Loeb, and Tseng's (2009) research suggested that aligning an ERM program with factors such as environmental uncertainty, industry competition, firm size and complexity, and monitoring by the board of directors leads to improved ERM performance.

Finally, di Serio et al. (2011) found that two main items facilitating ERM implementation in three award-winning Brazilian companies were leadership support and the use of a multifunctional team to implement ERM. Conversely, Arena et al. (2010) found that an ERM program that lacks leadership commitment may be perceived by the organization as an additional regulatory compliance activity. Aabo et al. (2005) noted additional implementation factors, including the assistance of a consultant, an ERM workshop to prioritize organizational risks, development of a written ERM policy and framework, linking of risk to organizational objectives, and identification of local managers to champion the program.

These findings support the need to adapt the ERM program to fit the culture and business processes at an organization. Moreover, they illustrate the importance of clearly outlining the purpose of ERM and educating employees on the goals of the ERM program. The evidence also points out that leadership commitment is required for implementing an ERM program. Furthermore, looking at the aggregate findings in this area highlight that implementing ERM requires the application of sound management practices. Consequently, although ERM is a distinct organizational activity, organizations should assess the management practices have worked when implementing other broad initiatives at the institution. An institution should next consider how it can use knowledge on previous initiatives to ascertain whether this can also enhance ERM implementation at the institution.

Organizational Culture

The evidence on the influence organizational culture has on ERM implementation is limited to findings from two studies. First, Kimbrough and Componation (2009) conducted a survey of 116 internal audit executives from various industries in the United States and 20 other countries. The survey revealed that organizations with organic cultures characterized by open, collaborative atmospheres in which employees were viewed as assets and required little direction were able to implement ERM faster and more effectively. Second, Silva, Wu, and Ojiako's (2013) case study of a Sri Lankan financial firm found that multiple cultures can coexist within an organization. Using Douglas's (1978) four risk culture dimensions (fatalism, hierarchy, individualism, and egalitarianism), the authors found the legal department heavily exhibited a hierarchy risk culture, while research personnel tended toward fatalism. Stock brokering staff members were individualistic, and accounting employees were egalitarian. Although the specific findings of culture types from this study cannot be extrapolated directly to similar departments in other organizational settings, it is reasonable to assume that large, complex organizations will have subcultures that tend to favor one or more of Douglas's risk culture dimensions. The limited information on the influence organizational culture has on ERM only suggests that culture does affect implementation. However, how culture affects implementation remains unclear.

Change Agents

Several studies have examined the influence a change agent—often referred to as a CRO in the literature—can have on ERM implementation. Paape and Speklé (2012) surveyed 825 public and nonprofit organizations from the Netherlands and found a correlation between the presence of a CRO and audit committee and the level of ERM implementation. Silva et al.'s (2013) survey of employees at a financial service company found internal support for hiring a CRO, while Kimbrough and Componation (2009) suggested that the appointment of a CRO led to faster ERM implementation and more effective programs. Interestingly, Clyde-Smith's (2014) study found

128

differing views were held among senior leadership on the skill sets needed by the person charged with ERM oversight. Some suggested that the person should have strong strategic planning skills, while others argued for an audit background with strong risk management skills. Another simply thought the role should be filled by the chief operating officer (COO) and supported by the CFO.

Mikes (2008) identified four roles risk managers fulfill: (a) compliance champion, who presses for organizational fulfillment of regulatory requirements; (b) modeling expert, who implements entity-wide processes for risk assessment and aggregation; (c) strategic advisor, who provides expertise on high-level risk decisions; and (d) strategic controller, who integrates risk and performance measurements that are reliable and utilized by the organization (p. 9). Similarly, Mikes's (2009) research identified three types of risk officers: (a) a risk silo specialist, who focuses on measuring and assessing risk and the production of large reports on which senior leadership place little value; (b) a risk capital specialist, who supports risk-based performance measures that aggregate the institution's risks and set risk limits (this person also fails to gain senior leadership attention); and (c) the senior risk officer, who plays a devil's advocate role that challenges existing organizational assumptions. This requires that they address nonquantifiable risks involving strategic and reputational issues with senior leadership. Mikes (2009) added that those overseeing a truly holistic risk management process need significant knowledge of the business. However, only those that have information and agenda-setting responsibilities can exert influence on strategic decision making. Therefore, the evidence suggests the need for an ERM program champion with the authority and resources to implement ERM. Moreover, an organization needs to select a leader for ERM that matches the type of program the institution wants to develop.

Program Design

Several studies have investigated the design of ERM programs. Andersen (2010) surveyed business executives to determine whether there is an association between organizations that use central planning in conjunction with decentralized decision making, higher average economic performance, and lower variation in performance. The author found organizations that scored above the median for emphasizing central planning and decentralized decision making had significantly higher average performance and lower variation in performance.

This supported the author's proposition that central planning in conjunction with decentralized decision making can lead to more effective risk management. In addition to this empirical research, the author further supported his argument by discussing how this proposition is advocated for in the literature on strategic management. Moreover, the author provided evidence that existing ERM models that only emphasize central planning can be improved if they incorporate decentralized decision making in the process for assessing and responding to organizational risks. However, this presented a macro view of the topic and did not provide evidence directly related to whether this would hold true for ERM. Nonetheless, these findings are relevant for organizations in which decentralized decision making is common.

Mikes (2009) distinguished four forms of ERM. First, risk silo management is consistent with traditional approaches to risk management that rely heavily on risk quantification techniques and control approaches. Second, integrated risk management, a similar approach, aspires to aggregate the individual risk of the organization. Third, risk-based management takes a more performance-driven approach to risk management. Last, holistic risk management seeks to manage nonquantifiable risks and includes such methods as

131

scenario and sensitivity analysis and risk assessment. Mikes (2009) suggested that holistic ERM focuses on both quantifiable and nonquantifiable risks where risk numbers are viewed as trend indicators, and learning about the underlying profile of risk is privileged. This model is driven by a risk-based control imperative that views ERM as a "learning machine." Similarly, Arena et al. (2011) identified three types of ERM systems: (a) responsive systems, which are superficial and used for external conformance; (b) discursive systems, which involve central knowledge sharing but do not guide future actions; and (c) prospective systems, which allow managers the ability to plan proactively for future actions. Moreover, their case study of nine Italian companies found various levels of risk integration. For example, two of the firms had high levels of integration with ERM being an integral part of key business processes with the local risk managers reporting to the CRO. On the other hand, three firms with medium levels of integration were characterized as having two independent risk management systems, with one focused on corporate level risk, such as strategy and compliance, and another that emphasized operational risks at the project level. Finally, four firms demonstrated low integration due to disparate and independent risk management practices specific to a certain risk category. Hence, an organization needs to determine what type of ERM program it wants to develop and design the program accordingly. The type of program also affects the characteristics of the person(s) the organization should select to oversee the program.

Barriers to Implementation

Several authors noted inhibitors to ERM implementation. Gates's (2006) survey found the top five impediments to ERM were competing priorities, insufficient resources, lack of agreement on the benefits of ERM, challenges associated with organizational change, and the lack of ability to quantify soft risks. However, Gates noted these challenges were perceived as less significant at firms that had advanced ERM programs. Similarly, Kleffner et al.'s (2003) study of Canadian organizations found inhibitors to ERM implementation included organizational structure and culture, resistance to change, lack of qualified personnel, and the needs of existing internal control systems. Additionally, Arena et al. (2010) found that ERM programs that were framed as a rule-based approach to risk management created distance between the ERM program and managers accountable for treating risks. The authors also found ERM was poorly received in one utility company that had strong existing risk-specific programs coupled with limited uncertainty due to operations being highly controlled by regulations. Last, in a survey of Chinese construction firms, Zhao et al. (2015) identified inhibitors to ERM implementation include insufficient resources, lack of perceived value for ERM, view that ERM increases costs, unsupportive organizational culture, and ineffective ERM training.

Muralidhar (2010) conducted a multiple case study involving six oil and gas companies from the Middle East (Bahrain, Kuwait, Oman, Qatar, Saudi Arabia, and United Arab Emirates) from 2005 to 2010. The author found that existing ERM frameworks did not adequately address how to quantify risks, communicate and develop stable organizational risk tolerance levels, link risk management to business strategy, and address conflicts between people that manage individual risk and the proponents of ERM. The author subsequently identified challenges to ERM implementation in three key areas. First, top structural challenges included consistency in communicating risk, board members' lack of risk awareness, audit committees, existing corporate cultures, and linking risk to strategy. Second, operational challenges included ownership of risk, lack of risk awareness at lower organizational levels, communication of risk due to cultural differences, and risk identification and classification.

Third, technical challenges included data accuracy, risk measurement, identification of risk appetite tolerances, and risk assessment and modeling.

In Aabo et al.'s (2005) case study of a Canadian utility company that successfully implemented ERM, the authors noted that the company first tried to use a consultant to develop the ERM program. However, this did not provide a lasting impact and failed to generate institutional knowledge on ERM. Therefore, the company decided to have an internal person lead the ERM effort, which yielded success. Similarly, Fraser et al. (2008) found executive dissatisfaction with the use of consultants for implementing ERM due the generic approaches and singular perspectives they have of ERM. However, several executives did acknowledge that consultants can be helpful in getting the ERM program started and providing insight into existing ERM frameworks and best practices.

While Kallenberg's (2009) study of 20 Swedish firms focused on operational risks, the authors identified challenges with implementing risk management similar to those noted in studies on ERM. These challenges include risk perceptions, cultural hurdles, and the ability to communicate and measure risks. Tekathen and Dechow (2013), in their case study of a large German manufacturing company, noted the further

135

challenge that organizational members may high-jack the risk management process by pushing personal or departmental agendas as part of the ERM process. In study of ERM at a university system, Huber and Rothstein (2013) identified five key factors that influenced risk management practices. First, new risk management practices were significantly influenced by existing structures, practices, and cultures. Second, ambiguities existed about what risk is and methodologies for assessing risk. Third, metrics to track risk management performance were lacking. Fourth, political actors manipulated some risk assessment processes in order to advance preferred projects or transfer responsibility for risk to members that had less ability to resist. Fifth, universities found it difficult to translate system-wide risk management aspirations into practice at the individual university level. Di Serio et al. (2011) further found ERM implementation can be inhibited by a lack of knowledge of risk assessment processes and the long time it takes to implement programming. Consequently, there are multiple potential barriers to implementing an ERM program. Hence, an organization needs to be cognate of these obstacles, design the program to minimize the likelihood of them occurring, and actively take steps to address them should they arise. Table 4 summarizes the mechanisms that either facilitate or are barriers to ERM implementation.

Table 4

Mechanisms that Facilitate or are Barriers to ERM Implementation

	Mechanism	Number of studies	Authors
Facilitators	Clear definition of what ERM means for the organization and program purpose and goals	6	Aabo et al. (2005); Arena et al. (2010); Hallowell et al. (2013); Lundqvist (2014); Silva et al. (2013); Zhao et al. (2013)
	Consistent with the existing organizational culture, objectives, and management practices	4	Aabo, et al. (2005); Andersen (2014); Gordon, Loeb, & Tseng (2009); Hallowell et al. (2013); Zhao et al. (2013)
	Cross-functional implementation team	4	Arena et al. (2010); Blaskovich and Taylor (2011); Di Serio et al. (2011); Hallowell et al. (2013)
	Central coordination, local management of risks	3	Aabo et al. (2005); Andersen (2014); Clyde-Smith (2014)
	Consultant for program set-up	2	Aabo et al. (2005); Fraser et al. (2004)
	Dedicated change agent	2	Aabo et al. (2005); Zhao et al. (2013)
	Leadership support	2	Di Serio et al. (2011); Zhao et al. (2013)
	Integrating existing risk management practices into the ERM program	1	Arena et al. (2010)
	ERM frameworks	1	Gates et al. (2012)

	Leveraging risk as opportunities	1	Zhao et al. (2014a)
Barriers	Existing organizational culture and resistance to change	6	Clyde-Smith (2014); Gupta (2006); Kallenberg (2009); Kleffner et al. (2003); Muralidhar (2010); Zhao et al. (2015)
	Consultant for long-term implementation process	2	Aabo et al. (2005); Fraser et al. (2004)
	Lack of adapting ERM framework to organizational environment	2	Arena et al. (2010); Lundqvist (2014)
	Lack of consensus on program purpose and goals	2	Gates (2006); Huber & Rothstein (2013)
	Competing priorities	2	Gates (2006); Kleffner et al. (2003)
	Unclear program metrics	2	Huber & Rothstein (2013); Kallenberg (2009)
	Program used to advance personal or department interests	2	Huber & Rothstein (2013); Tekathen & Dechow (2013)
	Unclear ERM frameworks	2	Lundqvist (2014); Muralidhar (2010)
	Poor understanding of ERM	2	Arena et al. (2010); Zhao et al. (2015)
	Lack of leadership support	1	Arena et al. (2010)
	Rules-based approach	1	Arena et al. (2010)
	Long time to implement ERM	1	Di Serio et al. (2011)
	Lack of resources	1	Gates (2006)
	Failure to link risk management to the organization mission	1	Gupta (2006)

	Unqualified change agent	1	Kleffner et al. (2003)
	Lack of accountability for risks	1	Muralidhar (2010)
Either facilitator or barrier	Diverse approaches to evaluating risks	1	Arena et al. (2011)
	ERM influenced by existing structures, practices, and cultures	1	Huber & Rothstein (2013)

Decision-Making Processes

Several authors have identified the role decision-making processes have in ERM implementation. Mikes (2009) proposed two types of calculative cultures: (a) quantitative enthusiasts who have an idealistic view that risk is quantifiable and favor analytical methods over managerial judgment; and (b) those who are skeptical of purely viewing risks from a quantitative perspective, hold a more pragmatic view of the limitations of analytical methods, and lean more toward organizational learning approaches. In another study, Paape and Speklé (2012) found that the frequent use of quantitative risk assessment techniques and risk reporting resulted in higher levels of perceived risk management effectiveness. Moreover, Huber and Rothstein (2013) found risk management served a normative role by presenting a picture of "rational" organizational decision making that served to increase the legitimacy of risk management processes for internal and external stakeholders.

Although Gates et al. (2012) suggested the value of clear risk tolerances, Paape and Speklé (2012) found less support for the value of developing risk tolerance levels. Arena et al. (2011) found organizations used different approaches to evaluate risks, with some having overarching measures to capture the portfolio of risks faced by the entity. One of the firms studied used a qualitative approach based on the probability and impact of an event, while two used quantitative approaches tied to financial measures. However, the majority of the companies in their study did not have an overarching practice to evaluate all risks. Instead, high-level risks were analyzed using a qualitative risk assessment matrix, and lower level risks were evaluated using a wide range of independent methods specific to the risk. Interestingly, Arena et al. (2010) found that one organization that participated in the case study had success in making ERM risk measures relevant to managers by linking them to preexisting performance measurement criteria.

Mathrani and Mathrani's (2013) case study of a New Zealand high-tech manufacturing firm suggested that information technology systems aid in risk mitigation. The authors identified that information technology tools for enhanced risk mitigation included the use of representative models that provide standard and customizable reports and forms. A key issue noted was the need to allow staff the ability to access the data easily, even if in read-only form. This type of system allowed for improved decision-making since the organization could base decisions on well analyzed and high quality data. In addition, the authors showed that the information technology systems could be combined with such business practices as balanced scorecards and dashboards in order to track and monitor risk management activities. However, setting up these processes required that risk-mitigating strategies were first defined and communicated clearly.

Arena, Azzone, Cagno, Silvestri, and Trucco's (2014), in a case study of an Italian global oil and gas company, investigated evaluating risks from a resource-based perspective. In this model, primary processes that directly influenced customer satisfaction and secondary support processes were mapped against the company's value chain. This resulted in the identification of 465 different organizational capabilities that spanned four organizational levels. These capabilities were assessed in relation to risk mitigation and consequences at each organization level in three areas: (a) the impact

142

performance variation in one area had on another area, (b) whether the unavailability of a capability in one area impacted another, and (c) whether an event in one area had a global impact affecting multiple organizational levels. This approach allowed the organization to assess whether a problem was ordinary and only required limited and static mitigation measures, or if it was a more systemic issue that offered an opportunity to generate new knowledge that could improve the overall business process.

Blaskovich and Taylor (2011) conducted a case-controlled study using 70 Master of Business Administration students and 69 Master of Accounting students from two large public universities in the United States. The goal of the study was to determine if groups composed of members with financial backgrounds would prioritize financial risks over other risks of similar magnitude. As the authors hypothesized, groups composed of people with financial backgrounds ranked financial risk higher. Based on these results, the authors suggested that the functional composition of ERM groups charged with evaluating risks influenced risk priorities, and recommended cross-functional groups for risk assessments. Similarly, participants in Clyde-Smith's (2014) study suggested the need for a cross-functional team composed of people from diverse professional and organizational backgrounds to provide oversight and leadership for the ERM initiative at the institution studied.

Aabo et al. (2005) further found that top risks were subject to a more thorough assessment to identify the worst credible outcome that could occur over a defined period, usually 2-5 years. In addition, the company studied assigned accountability to a risk owner for the residual risk. The risk owner could either retain the risk as is or take steps to change the level of risk by avoiding it, reducing its likelihood or consequences, or transferring it. Additionally, the company used three criteria to determine funding priorities to control risk in relationship to achieving organizational objectives, including assessing the severity of the risk, the probability that it would result in an adverse event, and the adequacy of existing controls. Therefore, the evidence suggests that an organization needs to develop clear risks assessment processes and tolerance levels appropriate for the type of risk. Moreover, the institution needs to involve stakeholders from different functional areas in the risk assessment process. Table 5 summarizes the ERM decision-making mechanisms identified in the literature.

Table 5

Decision Making Facilitators and Barriers

	Mechanism	Number of studies	Authors
Facilitators	Risk identification, analysis, and response	2	Aabo et al. (2005); Zhao et al. (2013)
	Cross-functional groups	2	Blaskovich & Taylor (2011); Clyde-Smith (2014)
	Assess risks associated with business processes		Arena et al. (2014)
	Risk funding based severity and probability the risk will be realized and the adequacy of existing controls	1	Aabo et al. (2005)
	Clearly defined risk tolerance levels	1	Gates, Nicolas, & Walker (2012)
	Information technology systems	1	Mathrani & Mathrani (2013)
	Frequent use of quantitative risk assessment techniques	1	Paape & Speklé (2012)
Barriers	Inadequate and/or unclear risk assessment processes	4	Di Serio et al. (2011); Gates (2006); Huber & Rothstein (2013); Muralidhar (2010)

Organizational Learning

Hallowell et al. (2013) found that effective implementation required the integration of ERM into an organization through training, workshops, and formal documents. However, Gupta's

(2011) survey of large- and medium-sized India-based companies in the manufacturing and service sectors found over 60% of respondents did not think risk needed to be communicated to every employee in the company. Alternatively, Gates et al. (2012) suggested that ERM can increase knowledge on organizational objectives and risks, which can lead to improved performance due to more informed decision making and the communication of organizational risks. Additionally, Arnold et al. (2012) stated that strong ERM processes promote enhanced absorptive capacity between a firm and its business chain partner(s), thus enabling supply chain partners to share information and knowledge, which leads to increased competitive advantage. Similarly, a study of transnational alliance partners suggests that ERM's ability to reduce risks and enhanced understanding of risks between partners leads to increased trust and subsequently enhanced information sharing among partners (Arnold, Benford, Canada, & Sutton, 2014). The evidence on the role organizational learning plays in ERM implementation is limited. However, although limited, the evidence does suggest that an ERM program needs to consider how it will educate the campus community on the ERM program. Table 6 summarizes the ERM organizational learning mechanisms identified from the literature.

146

Table 6

Organizational Learning Facilitators and Barriers

	Mechanism	Number of studies	Authors
Facilitators	Workshops, training, and formal documents	4	Aabo et al. (2005); Arena et al. (2010); Hallowell et al. (2013); Muralidhar (2010)
	Communication	2	Gates et al. (2012); Zhao et al. (2014a)
	Increased absorptive capacity	2	Arnold et al. (2012); Arnold et al. (2014)
Barriers	Lack of communication on risks	2	Huber & Rothstein (2013); Muralidhar (2010)
	Lack of training	2	Gupta (2006); Zhao et al. (2015)

In sum, the factors influencing ERM implementation can be divided into seven categories: (a) management practices, (b) culture, (c) change agents, (d) program design, (e) implementation barriers, (f) decision making, and (g) organizational learning. The most robust information identified speaks to the management practices that facilitate or are barriers to ERM implementation. Top facilitators include having a clear definition of what ERM means for the organization, a well-defined purpose and goals for the program, designing the program to be consistent with the existing culture and management practices, and the use of a cross-functional implementation team. Evidence

147

also suggests that an organization needs to select a person to lead the ERM effort that has the skillset to implement the type of program the organization seeks to develop. Top barriers identified were the existing organizational culture and employee resistance to change. Evidence suggests the role culture, decision making, and organizational learning play in ERM implementation is important. However, the evidence on why these areas are important and how they contribute to ERM implementation is lacking.

Chapter 18: A Model for ERM Implementation in Complex Organizations

In this chapter, I outline a process for ERM implementation in complex organizations based on the empirical evidence derived from my review of scholarly research on ERM. As Figure 6 illustrates, the ERM adoption and implementation process is consistent with Leseure et al.'s (2004) model on adopting promising practices discussed in the introduction to this section of the book. Following this model, implementing ERM is a five-stage process consisting of the adoption decision, setup (designing the program), implementation, ramp-up, and integration with the existing business practices at the organization. This chapter begins with a discussion of the logic for adopting ERM at an organization and the implications for how the adoption decision influences the type of ERM program the organization implements. Next, I outline the key mechanisms that affect ERM implementation, ramping up the ERM program, and integrating ERM into the institution's routines and decision-making processes.

Factors Influencing ERM Adoption

The adoption stage encompasses events that lead to the decision to adopt ERM. The evidence on whether ERM can increase the financial performance of an organization is inconclusive, possibly due to the challenges of directly linking ERM with the overall financial performance of an organization. However, the literature showed the reasons organizations decide to adopt an ERM strategy fall into two categories: compliance and performance. Leseure et al. (2004) found that practices pushed on an organization by regulations, management, or external norms that do not address a perceived organizational need fail to result in performance improvements. Institutional push factors identified are consistent with desires to improve compliance through the adoption of ERM. Factors in this area include improved regulatory compliance and governance, meeting stakeholder expectations, and board of director and leadership aspirations for integrated risk management approaches. Leseure et al. (2004) also found organizations adopt new management practices to address what they refer to as institutional pull factors. These factors focus on addressing organizational problems and are more likely to lead to improvements in performance. Pull factors fall into the performance category and

150

include factors such as enhancing risk management capabilities, improving decision making, and better crisis management.

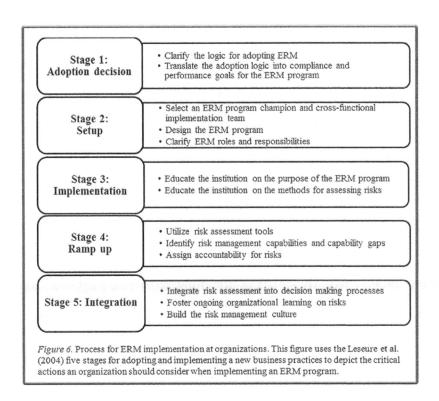

Figure 6. Process for ERM implementation at organizations. This figure uses the Leseure et al. (2004) five stages for adopting and implementing a new business practices to depict the critical actions an organization should consider when implementing an ERM program.

As such, organizations decide to adopt ERM to improve compliance and organizational performance. However, evidence suggests that organizations that only adopt ERM for compliance are less effective at ERM implementation (Arena et al., 2010). This finding is consistent with Leseure et al. (2004), who suggested business practices pushed onto

151

the organization to meet compliance needs rarely lead to performance improvements. Consequently, organizations that want to use ERM to improve performance need to make the case that they are adopting ERM to address challenges that could impede achieving the institution's strategic objectives. Examples in this area are improving risk management, decision-making, and building crisis management capabilities.

Therefore, at the adoption stage, the organization needs to clarify the logic for adopting an ERM strategy and translate this logic into preliminary compliance and performance goals for the ERM program. It is essential that the organization clarify why it is adopting ERM, since this affects the long-term trajectory of the program. For example, as Arena et al. (2010) suggested, organizations that adopt ERM primarily for compliance develop ERM programs that use defensive, control-based strategies focused on avoiding the negative consequences of risk. Organizations that view ERM strategically take an offensive stance, concentrating on managing risks in a manner that builds the ability to capitalize on opportunities and prevents illogical risk aversion. However, Arnold et al. (2012) suggested that ERM implementation normally progresses from compliance to minimize uncertainty associated with business processes to improving organizational performance so it can better capitalize on opportunities. Hence, improved compliance is a logical initial goal for an ERM program, with long-term goals emphasizing improving an organization's risk management, decision making, and crisis management processes.

Factors Influencing ERM Program Setup

The setup stage involves the decision to proceed with implementing ERM. This entails customizing the program to the organizational context and the identification and acquisition of resources to implement the ERM program. Leseure et al. (2004) suggested that shaping the program to fit the organization is critical to increasing the likelihood of program success. Findings from the literature support the need to design the ERM program to match the existing culture, mission, and management practices at the organization (Aabo et al., 2005; Andersen, 2014; Gordon et al., 2009; Hallowell et al., 2013; Zhao et al., 2013). Additionally, organizations that clearly define what ERM means for the organization and the program's purpose and goals (Aabo et al., 2005; Arena et al., 2010; Hallowell et al., 2013; Lundqvist, 2014; Silva et al., 2013; Zhao et al., 2013) are more successful at implementing ERM. Conversely,

153

the literature identified barriers to implementing ERM include not having a clear purpose and performance objectives and failing to adapt the program to the organizational environment (Arena et al., 2010; Gates, 2006; Huber & Rothstein, 2013; Kallenberg, 2009; Lundqvist, 2014; Muralidhar, 2010). Therefore, building a clear reason for implementing ERM at the organization is critical. The reasoning for adopting ERM needs to outline the adverse consequences the organization will incur if it fails in managing its risk. The organization also needs to explain how ERM can improve the institution's ability to achieve its strategic objectives. Moreover, the logic and implications for the ERM program need to explain the impact the program will have for key groups at the institution.

Program Champion and Implementation Team

The evidence suggests that setting up and implementing the ERM program requires an ERM champion and cross-functional implementation team. Although evidence suggests a consultant can be helpful to set up the ERM program, this study's findings suggest that using a consultant as a long-term strategy for ERM implementation is ineffective. This is because using a consultant fails to generate organizational learning (i.e., the consultant builds significant knowledge on the institution's risk instead of the organization; Aabo et al., 2005; Fraser et al., 2008). Thus, it is critical to select a program champion and implementation team to guide the implementation process. However, ERM's elevation of risk management from a middle management to a senior level function affects the type of change agent to lead the program. In addition, the type of ERM program an organization desires also influences the qualifications and characteristics of the person they should select to lead the effort. For example, Arena et al. (2010) noted that organizations that selected individuals to lead the implementation process whose focus was on compliance were less effective at embedding risk management into the organization's business processes. Hence, organizations need to identify a project champion that not only understands the intricacies of managing risks, but who also has a broad understanding of the complexities associated with implementing an organizational change initiative such as ERM. In addition, the organization should use a cross-functional team to implement the program (Arena et al., 2010; Blaskovich & Taylor, 2011; Di Serio et al., 2011; Hallowell et al., 2013). Members of this team need to be reflective of the broad set of operations and stakeholders at the institution. The team should also have members from senior leadership

155

recognized as credible leaders at the institution. The program champion and implementation team have responsibility for design and implementation of the ERM program. Two key items the champion and team need to consider when designing the program is how to structure the ERM program and the processes for assessing risks. The following discussion elaborates on these two items.

Program Design Factors

The evidence also showed the ERM program entails two main functional components: (a) a central coordination component and (b) a decentralized component for the local management of risks (Aabo et al., 2005; Andersen, 2014; Clyde-Smith, 2014). Central planning entails integrating the risk management activities of individual units with the overall goals for the organizations' mission, objectives, and risk management (Andersen, 2010). However, accountability and decision-making authority for managing risks remains at the local level, as long as it is consistent with the overall organizational tolerance for risk. Fraser et al. (2004) cautioned that the literature on ERM lacks "information on how to bring all the silos together—other than to say that a common reporting system and language

156

are important" (p. 74). Hence, it is critical that an organization clearly defines the role of the central planning unit and local groups charged with managing risks at the institution. Therefore, the ERM program needs a central governance function that: (a) clearly defines the purpose and goals for managing risks at the organization, (b) ensures local accountability for managing risks, (c) creates tools for assessing risks, and (d) educates local managers on the ERM program and tools for assessing risks. Additionally, local units need to be accountable for managing risks in their area(s) of responsibility and coordinating with other groups at the institution that are affected by the risk(s). Although local units are accountable for managing risks in their area of responsibility, the leadership at the organization is accountable for providing local units the resources necessary to control risks within the tolerance limits established by the institution.

Risk Assessment Factors

Another key component of ERM is the processes an organization uses to identify and evaluate risk. Therefore, an organization must determine the decision-making methods that are effective for assessing the types of risk at the institution. Yet, the evidence showed that

157

practitioners are frustrated by inadequate and unclear risk assessment processes (Di Serio et al., 2011; Gates, 2006; Huber & Rothstein, 2013; Muralidhar, 2010) and the lack of agreed-upon best practices for evaluating organizational risks. Indeed, Huber and Rothstein (2013) asserted that poor risk assessment processes may end up serving and justifying existing power structures and practices. Specifically, the authors identified three ways risk management can fail to challenge existing values and routines: (a) subjective and poor understanding of risk assessment measures, (b) subjective and fluid understandings of "acceptable" risks, and (c) ambiguous and poorly conceptualized risk identification processes. Additionally, the authors suggested that new risk management practices could disrupt existing responsibilities for risk, resulting in organizational struggles for blame attribution. Hallowell et al. (2013) also suggested that the type and characteristics of a risk influences how it will be managed and at what organizational level.

To explain methods for assessing risks at an organization, it is necessary to discuss how the type of risk affects an organization's processes for assessing risks. Defining risk at an organization can be especially challenging due to the diversity of stakeholders who differ on their views on what constitutes an acceptable risk and how much to invest in controlling risks. Kaplan and Mikes' (2012) three-category system introduced in Chapter 2 is an effective approach for classifying the types of risks organizations confront and the decision-making process to assess these risks. The three categories of risks in their system are: (a) preventable risks, (b) strategy risks, and (c) external risks (p. 55). Preventable risks are risks internal to the organization that arise in the course of conducting business such as the potential for unethical actions or safety hazards. Preventable risks lack strategic benefits but must be managed due to the adverse impact they can have on the organization. In contrast, strategy risks are risks an organization voluntarily takes to fulfill its mission. Examples include initiatives such as entering international educational markets or using private organizations to commercialize innovations developed at an organization. Strategic risks are not inherently undesirable, but require different strategies to manage than those used for preventable risks. Last, external risks surface from outside the organization, often beyond the control of the organization. External risks thus require that the organization develop processes to identify the threats and prepare contingency plans to manage them if they occur.

Sensemaking theory further explains the challenges and complexity   organizations encounter when assessing risks, especially those not well understood. For example, sensemaking theory illustrates that people go through a complex process to assess and respond to new events, in this case new risks (Weick, 1995). This is a social process where people consider how the risk affects them personally. Moreover, risks arise in an environment that continues to evolve and change. Thus, people seek to develop plausible understandings of the risks and, according to sensemaking theory, only fully understand risks retrospectively (Weick, 1995).

Consequently, the unique characteristics of risks along with the social and environmental dimensions identified from sensemaking theory affect how people assess risks. These factors help explain why some practitioners experience frustration with the processes used to assess risks. This is a particular concern with risk assessment processes that only use quantifiable measures to assess risks. Quantification may be reasonable for risks with measurable attributes. However, this is likely not the case for many of the complex risks an organization encounters. Moreover, Weick and Sutcliffe (2006) cautioned that simplifying events to fit preexisting mental frames can lead to the failure to notice unique characteristics and dimensions associated with new, unfamiliar events. Muralidhar (2010) added that fixed models for analyzing risks often fail to capture the flow of information inherent to a dynamic, changing, and evolving organizational environment. Consequently, a simple matrix for quantifying risk based on probability and consequences fails to capture the nuances associated with risks. This challenge is particularly salient when assessing the risks associated with new initiatives with which the organization does not have significant experience.

Two dimensions of risk often cited in the literature on ERM are risk appetite and tolerance. Risk appetite is the "amount and type of risk that an organization is willing to pursue and retain," and risk tolerance as an "organization's or stakeholder's readiness to bear the risk after risk response in order to achieve its objectives" (Zhao et al., 2013, p. 1207). For example, the Association of Governing Boards of Universities and Colleges and United Educators' (2009) survey of ERM in higher education found that fewer than 50% said their institutions understood their risk tolerances and factored them into decision-making processes. Hence, organizations need to provide people charged with assessing and managing risks clear information regarding how to assess risks in their operational area and the level of risk an organization is willing to retain in the pursuit of its strategic objectives.

Although organizations are making gains in how they manage risks, a gap continues to exist concerning how strategic risks are managed, primarily due to a lack of understanding how to evaluate and respond to them (Gates, 2006). Part of this may be due to an overemphasis on quantitative risk assessment methods. For example, risks associated with strategic initiatives can lack the historical data needed to understand their likelihood of occurring and the impact the risks have on realizing the initiative. However, a promising concept for assessing risks associated with strategic initiatives is to assess risks from a capabilities perspective. A capability perspective is also applicable to assessing external risks over which the organization has no or limited control. Arena et al. (2014) defined capabilities as an organization's "ability to leverage and transform its resources" (p. 180). Broadly speaking, organizational capabilities fall into four types: (a) capability to deliver services, (b) capability to support the delivery of services, (c) capability to learn new knowledge, and (d) capability to reconfigure existing resources to enhance existing competencies. According to Arena et al. (2014), building such capabilities allows the organization to endure better external and internal pressures that inhibit achieving strategic initiatives. In this context, an

162

organization assesses risks for their ability to inhibit the organizational capabilities necessary to achieve a strategic initiative.

Consider the following example: A university sets a strategic initiative to open a campus in a new foreign market. First, the university needs to determine the capabilities needed to deliver educational services in the new market. Next, it needs to assess the risks that could impede these capabilities. For instance, can the university navigate risks that inhibit its ability to secure capital and building permits necessary to construct facilities in the foreign country? Second, does the university have the necessary support services for this initiative? Does the university have competent knowledge of the legal, regulatory, and political systems of the new country? Third, how will the university learn from this experience to improve its capabilities to open additional new campus or to improve existing operations? Risks that could inhibit this type of learning could be the loss of key personnel or the loss of critical data from a cyber-attack or natural disaster that destroys a key information technology system. Hence, looking at risks in relation to the capabilities required to execute a strategic initiative shifts the discussion from the negative aspects of risks to one that focuses on building capabilities to address risks while also assessing how to enhance the organization's ability to act on opportunities.

163

Preventable risks relate to the operations at an organization. Although Kaplan and Mikes (2012) suggested preventable risks do not have strategic importance, as Kallenberg (2009) noted, mismanaged preventable risks can significantly influence the organization's ability to achieve its strategic objectives. As such, organizations need to determine how these risks threaten their ability to achieve their strategic objectives and whether further measures are required to control these risks. Additionally, strategic risks also transition into operational risks as the organization implements components of the new strategic initiative. Consider again the example of an organization with a strategic initiative to develop a campus on a new foreign market. As the organization puts this strategy into action, it will need to address preventable risks such as complying with safety and environmental standards. However, organizations that have already identified these risks and assessed existing capabilities to control them will be in a better position to manage these risks. This highlights the value of looking at strategic risks from a capabilities perspective.

Lastly, evidence suggests cross-functional teams can help overcome individual biases and provide a more balanced perspective on the significance of a risk (Blaskovich & Taylor, 2011; Clyde-Smith, 2014). For example, a team composed of individuals from one functional area at the organization will likely favor the allocation of resources to address risks in their area of responsibility. As such, a cross-functional team composed of people from multiple functional areas is more likely to evaluate and dedicate resources to address risks with an eye to ascertain how the risk affects the overall operations at the organization.

Factors Influencing ERM Implementation and Ramp-Up

Continuing along the process, the implementation phase is the launch of the program and focuses on actions with shorter completion periods. Leseure et al. (2004) stated that factors critical at this stage include a project champion, a well-designed program, training, supervisor reinforcement, and a developing commitment to the program. Evidence from the literature on ERM consistent with this stage includes having an ERM program champion, training and workshops, and leadership support. Next, the organization starts to use the promising practice (in this case ERM) during the ramp-up stage. At this stage, it is important to consider how ERM affects different groups and individuals versus using a one-size fits all approach.   This   requires tailoring goals to each level of the organization and communicating (including receiving feedback on the goals) with each level in the organization. Moreover, the process needs to be flexible and open to adapting the ERM program to meet the realities encountered during implementation. Findings from the research consistent with the ramp-up stage include central planning with decentralized decision making, communication, and diverse approaches to risk evaluation. The selection of the ERM program champion and implementation team along with considerations for designing the ERM program were discussed in the previous section. Therefore, this section focuses on findings in relation to operationalizing the ERM program.

Although organizations have unique cultures and organizational structures, the findings suggest that challenges with implementing ERM are neither unique to ERM nor higher education. For example, findings on ERM inhibitors include resistance to change (Clyde-Smith, 2014; Gupta, 2011; Kallenberg, 2009; Kleffner et al., 2003; Muralidhar, 2010) and not adapting the program to the organizational environment (Arena et al., 2010; Lundqvist, 2014). Additional inhibitors include poor information and communication (Kallenberg, 2009; Muralidhar, 2010) and the lack of consensus on goals (Gates, 2006; Huber &

Rothstein, 2013), priorities (Gates, 2006; Kleffner et al., 2003), and program metrics (Huber & Rothstein, 2013; Kallenberg, 2009). The inhibitors identified are consistent with those McCaskey (1982) identified with implementing a poorly designed program. McCaskey suggested these issues arise when organizations implement programs that are ill-conceived and not effectively communicated to the organization. This leads to what McCaskey (1982) refers to as ambiguous situations characterized by the factors listed in Table 7. Consequently, a well-designed ERM program can help prevent some of these issues from arising. However, decreasing ambiguity associated with ERM implementation also requires educating the campus community on the program.

Table 7

Characteristics of Ambiguous Situations

Characteristics
Lack of understanding the nature of the problem
Inability to effectively collect and categorize information
Multiple interpretations
Reliance on personal and professional values and political conflicts
Unclear and conflicting goals
Lack of resources
Situations that are vague and conflicting
Unclear roles and responsibilities
Lack of metrics
Failure to understand cause and effect relationships

Lack of clear definitions and logical lines of argument

Fluid participation in decision making

Note. Source: Adapted from McCaskey (1982), pp. 98-99.

Organizational Learning Factors

Ultimately, ERM is about changing how the organization thinks about the risk it faces, necessitating building organizational learning into the organization's ERM program. Unfortunately, findings from the literature on organizational learning were limited to the need for workshops, training, and formal documents (Aabo et al., 2005; Arena et al., 2010; Hallowell et al., 2013; Muralidhar, 2010) and improving how an organization communicates information on its risks and strategies for managing risks (Gates et al., 2012; Zhao et al., 2014a). An effective ERM program can build a stronger understanding of risk that leads to what Arnold et al. (2011) referred to as entrepreneurial alertness. This includes building the capacity to anticipate risks and opportunities and the ability to use this information to build a competitive advantage. Similarly, Arnold et al. (2012) suggested ERM could enhance an organization's ability to realize opportunities through strategic partnerships. In this scenario, ERM can help reduce the uncertainty found in the relationship between two or more organizations to promote joint problem solving and increase sharing of information.

Concepts on organizational learning discussed in Part 2 help to fill the gap in findings in this area. For example, Schein (2010) pointed out the need to create an environment that provides the psychological safety necessary for new learning. This necessitates building a convincing and positive vision for ERM, training on new risk management skills, using role models and support groups, and employing systems and structures that support new ways of thinking. Weick and Sutcliffe (2006) added that organizing an activity requires providing people with a "set of cognitive categories and a typology of action options" (p. 514). Scott (1992) further explained that organizations that view goals from an organizational learning perspective are less constrained by preexisting intentions and view goals as evolving through discovery. Thus, the ERM program needs to build educational activities that help people understand how to assess and respond to risks in their operational area. Moreover, the design of ERM educational programs should reflect the different learning needs of the various audiences at the institution. This requires multiple learning techniques tailored to address the diverse backgrounds of various groups at an organization.

Therefore, implementing the ERM program requires that the organization consider how it will educate the campus community on the ERM program. For some groups this may simply require making some groups aware of the ERM program and methods to report concerns on risks they observe. While other groups, such as those that will have a key role on evaluating and managing risks, require more extensive education on the organization's philosophy on managing risks and the processes employees can use to evaluate and manage risks. However, this requires creating educational programs that meet the learning needs of the various groups at the organization. Once staff are properly educated on the ERM program and risk assessment methods, the organization is positioned to ramp-up assessing its risks and current capabilities to control risks. This also facilitates identifying the group(s) who are accountable for managing certain risks at the institution and identifying if the organization needs additional risk management capabilities.

Factors Influencing ERM Integration

Last, the integration stage occurs after positive results gradually allow the new practice to become a part of the routine operations of the organization. Leseure et al. (2004) found that integrating new practices requires persistence in order to embed the practice into the organization's accepted knowledge base. However, evidence on how ERM can fully integrate into existing organizational practices is lacking. Indeed, only one study explicitly assessed the maturity of ERM. In Farrell and Gallagher's (2014) research, they employed the ERM maturity model developed by the Risk and Insurance Management Society to assess the level of ERM maturity at firms included in their study. The authors only found one organization of the 225 included the study had fully integrated ERM with existing practices at the organization. Most firms (41%) simply had ERM functions that showed repeatable application of various ERM processes. Factors considered in this model were whether an organization adopted an ERM approach to manage risks, established ERM processes, set risk tolerances, managed uncertainty, or built organizational resiliency and sustainability.

A concept that captures the characteristics of a fully integrated ERM program is organizational resiliency. Weick and Sutcliffe's (2007) five characteristics of a resilient organizations help to conceptualize what an integrated ERM program should look like. First, such programs have a preoccupation with identifying risks and see risk identification as an opportunity to improve processes. Second, resilient organizations are reluctant to simplify risk. Hence, merely identifying risks and subjectively assigning numerical probability and severity ratings is inadequate for understanding the risks faced by an organization. Third, organizational resiliency requires that the organization understand the operational challenges frontline personnel confront. This is of particular concern due to the continued effort to reduce operating costs at organizations. Fourth, organizations need to be committed to building resiliency through a constant effort to identify risks that could cause systems to fail. Last, organizations need to build structures that place decision-making authority in the hands of the people most knowledgeable of the process. Building resiliency as part of the ERM program not only helps to protect the institution, but also helps to build confidence in the organization's ability to manage risks. This can translate into an increased ability to capitalize on opportunities. An effective ERM program will identify areas an organization can strengthen in order to increase their capability to take on projects with risks their competitors may be wary of undertaking. Moreover, the avoidance of projects that overexpose an organization can prevent drains on resources that prevent seizing opportunities due to the tie-up of resources.

In sum, the framework presented in this chapter identified the factors associated with adopting an ERM strategy. Although this framework portrayed operationalizing ERM as a sequential process, implementing ERM at an organization is likely to be a more iterative process. Hence, the activities discussed in this chapter above may occur contemporaneously. The empirical evidence supporting the process for ERM implementation at organization has been located in companies from multiple industries and geographic settings. This diversity suggests both the findings and the ERM process are indeed transferable to other settings.

Part 4: Seven Principles for ERM Adoption and Implementation

In the final section of this book, I first present seven principles for ERM adoption and implementation derived from both the findings of the research literature on ERM and my professional experience. Incorporating these principles into an organization's ERM program will enhance the probability that the program will be successful. Lastly, in the closing chapter, I provide some final thoughts on implementing ERM along and discuss implications for management theory and future research on ERM.

Chapter 19: The Seven Principles

The research reviewed in this book highlights the challenges organizations face with changing how they manage risks. ERM shifts risk management from an operational level function to one that also considers risk within the broader context of the overall management and mission of the organization. Although the literature's findings imply that organizations are beginning to employ management science concepts to better ERM implementation, the application of such practices is still in its infancy. Therefore, in this chapter, I outline a set of principles for ERM implementation grounded in concepts from management theory and findings from studies on ERM. In sum, effective ERM implementation requires integrating risk management into an organization's business practices and decision-making processes to manage risks within tolerated limits and improve the capability of the organization to capitalize on opportunities. Application of these principles will improve the likelihood an organization will be effective at ERM implementation. Table 8 provides an overview of the seven principles I believe are integral in ERM implementation.

Table 8

Principles for ERM Adoption and Implementation

Principle	Statement
Principle 1	Adopt an ERM strategy to improve organizational performance.
Principle 2	Clarify the purpose and goals of the ERM program for each major operating unit and at each organizational level.
Principle 3	Design the ERM program to reflect the organization's culture and existing business practices.
Principle 4	Select a program champion and implementation team that has the skill sets needed to implement the type of ERM program the organization desires.
Principle 5	Develop and utilize decision-making methodologies appropriate for evaluating the type of risk.
Principle 6	Use ERM to stimulate organizational learning on risks and the capabilities the organization has to control risk.
Principle 7	Use ERM to build a risk management culture that reflects the characteristics of resilient organizations.

Principle 1: Adopt ERM to Improve Performance

To maximize the impact of ERM requires that organizations adopt ERM (i.e., decide to use an ERM strategy to manage risks) to improve performance. Examples of performance issues organizations seek to address by adopting ERM include improving risk management practices, decision-making processes, and crisis planning. Although some organizations may adopt ERM simply to improve compliance, evidence suggests that those who adopt ERM primarily to improve compliance end up with programs that rely heavily on control strategies (e.g., auditing and enforcement of rules). Such programs are likely to meet resistance and are unlikely to integrate risk management into the culture and business processes at the organization. Moreover, as Leseure et al. (2004) suggested, management practices pushed on an organization by regulations or management has limited effects on performance. However, Leseure et al. found that adopting management practices that address real problems are more likely to result in improved performance. Hence, an organization needs to stress how ERM will help solve challenges the organization faces. Moreover, the organization should promote how implementing an ERM strategy to improve performance in areas such as risk management, decision-making, and crisis planning helps it realize its strategic objectives. Therefore, Principle 1 is: *Adopt an ERM strategy to improve organizational performance.*

Principle 2: Clarify the Purpose and Goals of the ERM Program

Simply stating an organization is adopting ERM to improve performance is insufficient. The evidence from the literature stresses the importance of clarifying the purpose for adopting an ERM strategy. In fact, clearly defining the purpose and goals for ERM at the organization was identified as the top method for improving ERM implementation (Aabo et al., 2005; Arena et al., 2010; Hallowell et al., 2013; Lundqvist, 2014; Silva et al., 2013; Zhao et al., 2013). This necessitates establishing performance goals for the ERM program for each major operating unit and organizational level. Senior leadership goals need to focus on strategic risks and external threats whereas operational unit goals focus on preventable risks. Indeed, ERM programs often begin by addressing the compliance goals. Hence, it is reasonable for an organization to set compliance improvement as an initial ERM goal. However, integrating ERM into the organization's business practices and decision-making processes require establishing goals for the ERM program that improve organizational performance. Goals in this area should focus on: (a) improving risk management processes (Arnold et al., 2012; Clyde-Smith, 2014; Fraser et al., 2008; Gates, 2006; Hallowell et al., 2013; Kanhai et al., 2014), (b) improving decision-making processes (Arena et al., 2011; Fraser et al., 2008; Gates et al., 2012; Hallowell et al., 2013; Zhao et al., 2015), and (c) enhancing crisis management capabilities (Fraser et al., 2008; Hallowell et al., 2013; Seik et al., 2011). Therefore, Principle 2 is: *Clarify the purpose and goals of the ERM program for each major operating unit and organizational level.*

Principle 3: Design ERM to Reflect the Organization's Culture and Routines

The evidence suggests that designing the ERM program to reflect the existing organizational culture and management practices improves ERM implementation (Aabo et al., 2005; Andersen, 2014; Gordon, Loeb, & Tseng, 2009; Hallowell et al., 2013; Zhao et al., 2013). Conversely, ERM programs that are not compatible with the existing organizational culture along with resistance to change were found to be the top barriers to ERM implementation (Clyde-Smith, 2014; Gupta, 2006; Kallenberg, 2009; Kleffner et al., 2003; Muralidhar, 2010; Zhao et al., 2015). Although ERM aspires to change the culture regarding how an organization manages risk, realizing this long-term goal requires that ERM be compatible with the culture and existing business practices at the organization. This is of particular importance at the inception of the program.

Evidence from the literature suggests ERM programs have two main functional areas: (a) a central coordination function, and (b) local units with accountability for managing risks (Aabo et al., 2005; Andersen, 2014; Clyde-

179

Smith, 2014). Examples of roles for the central coordination function include the aggregation and reporting of data on risks, identifying units accountable for risks, developing risk assessment tools, clarifying risk tolerance levels, and educating employees on the ERM program. Designing the central coordination function requires determining how to integrate ERM into the existing organizational structure and business processes. Local accountability for managing risks is critical since these units have the best knowledge on how to manage the risks in their areas of responsibility. However, organizations need to support local efforts to manage risks within the tolerance levels established by the organization. Furthermore, the organization needs to evaluate existing performance measures and reward systems to determine how to use these structures to encourage the effective management of risks at the local level. Therefore, Principle 3 is: *Design the ERM program to reflect the organization's culture and existing business practices.*

Principle 4: Select a Program Champion and Implementation Team with the Proper Skills

The evidence supports that a cross-functional implementation team (Arena et al., 2010; Blaskovich & Taylor, 2011; Di Serio et al., 2011; Hallowell et al., 2013) and, to a lesser degree, a dedicated change agent (Aabo et al., 2005; Zhao et al., 2013) facilitates ERM implementation. The cross-functional implementation team needs to be comprised of employees representing key functional areas at the organization. The team should have a mix of senior leadership well versed in the strategic direction of organization along with managers and employees from operational units responsible for managing risks. Members of the team should be recognized as leaders at the organization. The type of ERM program affects whom the organization should select as the program champion. For example, organizations that only seek to address compliance through the ERM program may be best served by choosing a person with a strong compliance and auditing background. While those that seek broader performance improvements from the ERM program require a person that understands risk management and who has general background of the critical management and programmatic functions of the organization. In addition to understanding risk management, the program champion should have a substantial understanding of management concepts in areas such as change management, decision making, and organizational learning. Therefore, Principle 4 is: *Select a program champion and implementation team that has the skill sets needed to implement the type of ERM program the organization desires.*

Principle 5: Use Decision-Making Methodologies Appropriate for the Risk

March (1994) suggested that effective decision-making processes can alleviate uncertainty and ambiguity and serve as a vehicle for forming meaningful interpretations of unclear situations or events. Indeed, the evidence showed that inadequate and unclear risk assessment processes are a key barrier to evaluating risks effectively (Di Serio et al., 2011; Gates, 2006; Huber & Rothstein, 2013; Muralidhar, 2010). Hence, organizations need to design risk assessment tools appropriate for the type of risk and operating unit evaluating risks. For example, operational units charged with managing safety risks may only require checklists to evaluate if safety hazards are being properly controlled in their area of responsibility. Whereas groups looking at strategic risks, such as entry into a new business market or partnership, may require facilitated discussions on the risks these new ventures present and whether the organization has the existing capabilities to control these risks within acceptable tolerance levels. Last, organizations need to establish metrics for the ongoing monitoring of risks. This is critical to alerting leadership when risks elevate above the tolerance levels established by the organization. Therefore, Principle 5 is: *Develop and utilize decision-making methodologies appropriate for evaluating the type of risk.*

Principle 6: Stimulate Organizational Learning on Risk

Evidence on generating organizational learning on risk has been limited to workshops, training, and formal documents (Aabo et al., 2005; Arena et al., 2010; Hallowell et al., 2013; Muralidhar, 2010). However, organizations can generate crucial knowledge on risks that can impede the ability to achieve their strategic objectives. Moreover, understanding the organization's existing capabilities to control risks within tolerance levels allows the organization to determine where to build additional risk control capabilities. Increased institutional knowledge on risks can improve understanding on the risk interdependencies and therefore facilitate discussions on holistically managing these risks. Furthermore, understanding existing risk management capabilities enhances an organization's ability to determine which opportunities to pursue and can prevent unreasonable aversions to risk. Therefore, Principle 6 is: *Use ERM to stimulate organizational learning on risks and the capabilities the organization has to control risk.*

Principle 7: Build Organizational Resiliency Capabilities through ERM

The evidence identified the key motive for adopting an ERM strategy is to improve the risk management culture at an organization (Arnold et al., 2012; Clyde-Smith, 2014; Fraser et al., 2008; Gates, 2006; Hallowell et al., 2013; Kanhai et al., 2014). To revisit, Cooper et al. (2013) defined risk culture as

> a pattern of basic assumptions that the group learned as it identified, evaluated, and managed its internal and external risks that has worked well enough to be considered valid, and therefore to be taught to new members as the correct way to perceive, think, and feel in relation to those risks. (p. 65)

However, this definition fails to highlight the characteristics of an effective risk management culture. As previously discussed, resilient organizations illustrate a culture that is effective at managing risk. Cultural attributes of resilient organizations include: (a) preoccupation with failure,

184

(b) reluctance to accept simplification, (c) sensitivity to operations, (d) assignment of decision-making authority to people knowledgeable of the process, and (e) commitment to resilience (Weick & Sutcliffe, 2007). Hence, organizations need to build a culture that encourages reporting risks and learning from failures to improve processes. The culture also should be reluctant to accept assessments of risks that fail to look into systemic factors that contribute to generating risk. Organizations also need to be conscious of the challenges operational units face managing risks. This requires providing the resources needed for operational units to control risks that threaten the ability to achieve the organization's strategic objectives. This also entails assigning decision-making authority to people who are the most knowledgeable on the risk. Last, organizations must acknowledge that no system is perfect and, thus, that they need to identify and learn from failures constantly. Therefore, Principle 7 is: *Use ERM to build a risk management culture that reflects the characteristics of resilient organizations.*

Commentary

These seven principles outline the critical factors that influence effective ERM implementation at organizations. However, these principles should not be considered all-inclusive. In addition, implementation of a broad organizational initiative such as ERM is a complex process that requires a long-term commitment by leadership. Moreover, new challenges and opportunities will emerge throughout the implementation process. Consequently, organizations should seek feedback actively from employees on how to improve ERM, and be open to adapting ERM to meet the new realities encountered during implementation.

ERM is a strategy to managing the broad range of risk at an organization. As such, implementing an ERM program is similar to implementing other significant management initiatives. Indeed, the first four principles are applicable to a wide range of management initiatives. For example, most organizations implement new management programs to improve performance. Also, clarifying the program's purpose and goals, designing the program to reflect the exiting organizational culture, and properly selecting a program champion and implementation team are common best practices for implementing a new management program.

In addition, when considering the methodologies, the organization will use to decide which risks to prioritize for treatment requires using decision-making processes that are effective at identifying and evaluating risks and are consistent with how the organization currently makes decisions. ERM should also be used to stimulate organizational learning and building the organization's risk management capabilities. Last, it is ultimately up to leadership to decide the type of risk management culture they want to create at the organization. The research and opinion of this author suggests that the characteristics of resilient organizations reflect the cultural dimensions of an effective ERM program.

Chapter 20: Concluding Remarks

The literature shows that ERM programs have begun to employ concepts from the management sciences; however, the application of these concepts is not complete nor is it employed in a holistic manner. In this book, I illustrated how management theories utilized in the evidence base apply to understanding ERM. For example, findings related to the influence of the external and internal environment on ERM adoption and implementation reflect concepts from institutional theory, while findings related to the ongoing, dynamic, and long-term process involved in implementing ERM speak to theories on change management. Challenges related to risk identification and assessment correlated to the concepts outlined in sensemaking theory, whereas the challenges with fostering understanding an institution's risk and risk control capabilities spoke to theories on organizational learning. Therefore, this discussion demonstrates the value of applying concepts from the management sciences to explain ERM program implementation. A factor necessitating the application of management science theory is that ERM extends risk management by making the management of risks an organizational governance process requiring senior leadership. As a comprehensive organizational program, ERM requires insight from management theories in areas such as change management, decision making, and organizational learning. The following is an overview of how each of the theories in these areas contributes to understanding ERM, along with the main findings from the literature.

Overview of the Evidence Base: Theory and Practice

Legitimacy and institutional theory theories advance understanding of why an organization would adopt ERM. Legitimacy theory explains motives for adopting ERM while institution theory illuminates how the rationale for adopting ERM influences the type of program the institution implements. Early studies on ERM focused on financial value; however, profit motives may not be the key driver for ERM adoption at less profit-orientated organizations such as higher education institutions. As such, legitimacy theory helps to explain other factors that motivate the adoption of ERM at organizations. To reiterate, legitimacy theory is "a generalized perception or assumption that the actions of an entity are desirable, proper, or appropriate within some socially-constructed system of norms, values, beliefs, and definitions" (Suchman, 1995, p. 574). The critical factor affecting the legitimacy of an organization's actions is the perceptions

189

internal and external stakeholders have of these activities (Walker, 2010). Thus, in an organizational setting with a multitude of influential internal and external stakeholders, senior leadership may be motivated to adopt ERM to demonstrate the institution is utilizing an accepted practice to manage risks.

Similarly, institutional theory illustrates how pressure from governmental agencies, the public, and professional norms influences organizations (Wicks, 2001). Consistent with institutional theory, research on ERM suggests that organizations that adopt ERM solely to improve compliance rely heavily on the regulatory element of institutional theory. Consequently, these organizations develop ERM programs that are separate from the core processes of the organizations. As such, compliance-focused ERM programs rely on coercive techniques that generate defensive responses. In contrast, organizations that adopt ERM to improve organizational performance are likely to employ management practices consistent with the normative and culture-cognitive elements of institutional theory. Hence, theoretical work on ERM can benefit from exploring how the normative and culture-cognitive elements of institutional theory can advance strategies for ERM implementation.

As a process for managing the overall risk at an institution, ERM implementation often occurs over an extended timeframe, involves multiple organizational actors, and is an ongoing iterative process. Hence, ERM implementation encounters challenges similar to those found with implementing organizational change initiatives. Examples include conflict with the existing organizational culture, resistance to change, lack of consensus on program purpose and goals, lack of leadership support and resources, and using an unqualified change agent. Therefore, theories on change management illustrate that ERM implementation is an ongoing process entailing both planned change and the need to recognize opportunities to capitalize on local innovation throughout the implementation process (Orlikowski & Hofman, 1997). Moreover, consistent with Schein's (2010) model for managed cultural change, successful ERM implementation involves three stages of change. First, the institution needs to create motivation for using ERM to manage risks. Second, using ERM to manage risks requires that the organization educate staff on the concepts and practices associated with ERM. Last, the organization needs to take action to help staff internalize the new concepts, meanings, and standards associated with using ERM to manage risks.

In his review of sensemaking theory, Weick (1995) stated that the level of ambiguity (unclear meaning) an organization faces is due to two critical factors: (a) the amount of influence the environment has on the organization and (b) the level of structure in an organization's systems. Weick (1995) used these criteria to depict organizations as rational, natural, or open systems. Rational systems are highly structured organizations that focus on achieving defined goals. Natural systems have informal structures and less defined goals that are driven by the shared interests of stakeholders. Last, open systems involve shifting coalitions that negotiate goals and are highly influenced by environmental factors. The diverse structures, multitude of stakeholders, and strong external influences common to organizations typify the characteristics outlined in open systems. Weick (1995) posited that organizations reflective of open systems must deal with high levels of ambiguity, which in turn necessitates significant levels of sensemaking. However, existing ERM frameworks propose implementation strategies that are more applicable in rational systems. As such, they are less compatible with organizations that are more reflective of natural or open systems. Therefore, studying ERM implementation at organizations can benefit from the application of concepts found in the scholarly research on natural or open organizational environments.

The evidence showed practitioner dissatisfaction with existing ERM processes for evaluating risks, especially for risks that lack quantifiable attributes (Di Serio et al., 2011; Gates, 2006; Huber & Rothstein, 2013; Muralidhar, 2010). This finding is consistent with the limits scholars have noted regarding rational decision-making models. Such models assume decision makers have complete and accurate information and fully understand the concerns of the parties affected by the decision (Bazerman & Moore, 2009). Therefore, since these conditions are not likely to exist, new methods for assessing and understanding risks are needed. Sensemaking theory provides a deeper explanation of how organizations assess risks. Sensemaking theory means, literally, "the making of sense" (Weick, 1995, p. 4), and is a process that illustrates the social and retrospective nature of how organizations understand and respond to new phenomena such as risk. Sensemaking theory highlights that such a process involves understanding how the risk affects a person's identity, occurs within an evolving social context, is retrospective, and requires plausible explanations.

The literature provided limited evidence on how organizations leverage organizational learning as part of their ERM program. Indeed, the findings

193

are predominately limited to the need to offer training and workshops on ERM (Aabo et al., 2005; Arena et al., 2010; Hallowell et al., 2013; Muralidhar, 2010). Consequently, understanding ERM implementation at organizations is enhanced by applying concepts on organizational learning. A promising concept found in this area is absorptive capacity, the collective abilities of an organization to recognize the value of new information and utilize it for business purposes (Sun & Anderson, 2010). In this case, ERM can build the absorptive capacity between partnering organizations via increased understanding of risks, and trust that each organization has reasonable measures to control risks (Arnold et al., 2012, 2014).

Studies on ERM have advanced from those based on publicly available financial data to longitudinal studies of organizations that have implemented ERM. Indeed, this discussion illustrates that research on ERM implementation can benefit from the application of the management theories previously discussed. Enterprise risk management research has also expanded beyond the financial and insurance sectors to a wide range of industries and geographical settings. As such, ERM can serve as a topical area for exploring theoretical explanations on organizational phenomena such as organizational change and decision making under conditions of high levels of uncertainty and ambiguity. Studying ERM in the higher education environment adds the element of diverse and multiple organizational cultures with powerful internal and external actors. Hence, ERM implementation is a fruitful area for studying organizational change initiatives and decision making in complex organizational environments. Therefore, both theory and practice can benefit from using the management theories outlined in this research to advance research and theory development on ERM in higher education institutions and other complex organizational settings.

Recommendations for Future Research

Future research is needed to test the findings and principles already established in the literature and through my systematic review. For example, an action research approach could test the findings and management implications derived from research. Action research involves the active collaboration between research and collaborators in order to diagnose and develop solutions to problems encountered by practitioners (Holter & Schwartz-Barcott, 1993). Hence, using an action research methodology would offer the opportunity for additional research on how findings from the literature influence ERM implementation in complex organizations.

Conducting a multiple case study to determine how the characteristics and culture at an organization influence ERM implementation may also be productive. In a higher education setting, Birnbaum's (1988) classification of organizations (i.e., collegial, bureaucratic, political, and anarchical) could form the basis for differentiating organizations by their primary mode of operation. For example, the study could first identify organizations with ERM programs for each type of institution as defined by Birnbaum. Next, the research could entail conducting a case study at each type of institution to tease out differences in ERM implementation between the types of institutions. Knowledge gained from this type of study can aid in designing ERM strategies more specific to the organizational environment.

Research is also needed to determine which risk assessment techniques are applicable to the different types of risks organizations encounter. A systematic review of the literature on risk assessment techniques and decision making may be an effective means for conducting this research. Another topic for future research is whether ERM builds organizational resiliency. In this instance, Weick and Sutcliffe's (2007) five characteristic of high-reliability organizations introduced in Chapter 2 (i.e., preoccupation with failure, reluctance to accept simplification, sensitivity to operations, commitment to resilience, and deference to expertise) could form the criteria for assessing resiliency levels at organizations. The research could also identify organizations with mature ERM programs (see Farrell & Gallagher, 2014 for an ERM maturity assessment model) and organizations without ERM programs. Next, the research could assess whether organizations with mature ERM programs exhibit statistically significant differences in organizational resiliency.

Furthermore, research is needed to understand the value of ERM at organizations. The findings on whether ERM contributes to increasing the financial value of an organization are mixed. This may be due to the studies' reliance on publicly available financial data and/or failure to factor in the quality of the ERM programs at the organizations examined. This could also be due to the studies defining value in financial terms only instead of the overall wellbeing of the organization and other indicators of success. Therefore, it is not clear whether organizations should expect to see improved financial performance from implementing ERM. Similar to the study suggested on organizational resiliency, a study on financial performance could identify organizations with mature ERM and compare their financial performance to organizations that do not have an ERM program. Research could also investigate other metrics for evaluating whether ERM is beneficial to organizations.

Final Thoughts

A successful ERM program is one in which an organization effectively considers the risks that could impede the institution's ability to achieve its strategic objectives. Additionally, organizations that understand their risk profile and have measures in place to control risks are in a better position to capitalize on opportunities. However, how an organization achieves these outcomes through the application of an ERM strategy is unclear. Therefore, in this book, I explored why an organization would decide to adopt an ERM strategy, along with the critical success factors for implementing ERM in higher education. In doing so, I showed the value of utilizing concepts from change management, decision making, and organizational learning to inform ERM implementation. These concepts, in combination with the evidence based on ERM in organizations, was synthesized to explain a model or framework for ERM implementation, along with a set of seven principles that will increase the likelihood for success. In sum, organizations that adopt ERM to improve performance at the institution in areas such as risk management, decision making, and crisis planning are more likely to develop impactful ERM programs. Second, organizations must clarify the purpose of the ERM program for each operating unit and organizational level at the institution. Third, organizations need to design the ERM program to reflect the culture and business practices at the organization. Fourth, the ERM program needs an effective champion and cross-functional implementation team. Fifth, ERM requires multiple risk assessment methodologies that match the type of risk under evaluation. Sixth, the ERM program needs to build the institution's understanding of the risks that can impede achieving its strategic objectives and the capabilities it has to control these risks. Finally, ERM is a tool for building a risk management culture that reflects the characteristics of resilient organizations.

References

Aabo, T., Fraser, J. S., & Simkins, B. J. (2005). The rise and evolution of the chief risk officer: Enterprise risk management at Hydro One. *Journal of Applied Corporate Finance, 17*(3), 62–75. doi:10.1111/j.1745-6622.2005.00045.x

Abraham, J. M. (2013). *Risk management: An accountability guide for university and college boards.* Washington, DC: AGB Press.

The Advisory Board. (2008). *Implementing enterprise risk management: Customer research brief.* Washington, DC: Author. Retrieved from http://www.eab.com/Research-and-Insights/Business-Affairs-Forum/Custom/2008/09/Implementing-Enterprise-Risk-Management

Andersen, T. J. (2010). Combining central planning and decentralization to enhance effective risk management outcomes. *Risk Management, 12*(2), 101–115. doi:10.1057/rm.2009.13

Arena, M., Arnaboldi, M., & Azzone, G. (2010). The organizational dynamics of enterprise risk management. *Accounting, Organizations, & Society, 35,* 659–675. doi:10.1016/j.aos.2010 .07.003

Arena, M., Arnaboldi, M., & Azzone, G. (2011). Is enterprise risk management real? *Journal of Risk Research, 14*(7), 779–797. doi:10.1080/13669877.2011.571775

Arena, M., Azzone, G., Cagno, E., Silvestri, A., & Trucco, P. (2014). A model for operationalizing ERM in project-based operations through dynamic capabilities. *International Journal of Energy Sector Management, 8*(2), 178. doi:10.1108/IJESM-09-2012-0008

Argyris, C. (1976). Single-loop and double-loop models in research on decision making. *Administrative Science Quarterly, 21*(3), 363–375. doi:10.2307/2391848

200

Argyris, C. (1980). Making the undiscussable and its undiscussability discussable. *Public Administration Review, 40*(3), 205-213. doi:10.2307/975372

Arnold, V., Benford, T., Canada, J., & Sutton, S. G. (2011). The role of strategic enterprise risk management and organizational flexibility in easing new regulatory compliance. *International Journal of Accounting Information Systems, 12*(3), 171-188. doi:10.1016/j .accinf.2011.02.002

Arnold, V., Benford, T. S., Hampton, C., & Sutton, S. G. (2012). Enterprise risk management as a strategic governance mechanism in B2B-enabled transnational supply chains. *Journal of Information Systems, 26*(1), 51-76. doi:10.2308/isys-10253

Arnold, V., Benford, T. S., Hampton, C., & Sutton, S. G. (2014). Enterprise risk management: Re-conceptualizing the role of risk and trust on information sharing in transnational alliances. *Journal of Information Systems, 28*(2), 257-285. doi:10.2308/isys-50812

Association of Governing Boards of Universities and Colleges & United Educators. (2009). *The state of enterprise risk management at colleges and universities today.* Retrieved from http://www.agb.org/reports/2009/state-enterprise-risk-management-colleges-and-universities-today

Baranoff, E., Harrington, S. E., & Niehaus, G. R. (Eds.). (2005). *Risk assessment* (1st ed.). Malvern, PA: The Institutes.

Baron, R. A., & Ensley, M. D. (2006). Opportunity recognition as the detection of meaningful patterns: Evidence from comparisons of novice and experienced entrepreneurs. *Management Science, 52*(9), 1331-1344. doi:10.1287/mnsc.1060.0538

Bazerman, M. H., & Moore, D. A. (2009). *Judgment in managerial decision making.* Hoboken, NJ: John Wiley & Sons.

Beach, L. R., & Connolly, T. (2005). *The psychology of decision making: People in organizations* (2nd ed.). Thousand Oaks, CA: Sage.

201

Beasley, M., Clune, R., & Hermanson, D. R. (2005). Enterprise risk management: An empirical analysis of factors associated with the extent of implementation. *Journal of Accounting & Public Policy, 24*(6), 521–531. doi:10.1016/j.jaccpubpol.2005.10.001

Beasley, M., Pagach, D., & Warr, R. (2008). Information conveyed in hiring announcements of senior executives overseeing enterprise-wide risk management processes. *Journal of Accounting, Auditing, & Finance, 23*(3), 311–332. doi:10.2139/ssrn.916783

Bigley, G. A., & Roberts, K. H. (2001). The incident command system: High-reliability organizing for complex and volatile task environments. *Academy of Management Journal, 44*(6), 1281–1299. doi:10.2307/3069401

Birnbaum, R. (1988). *How colleges work: The cybernetics of academic organization and leadership.* San Francisco, CA: John Wiley & Sons.

Bisel, R. S., & Arterburn, E. N. (2012). Making sense of organizational members' silence: A sensemaking-resource model. *Communication Research Reports, 29*(3), 217–226. doi:10.1080/08824096.2012.684985

Blaskovich, J., & Taylor, E. Z. (2011). By the numbers: Individual bias and enterprise risk management. *Journal of Behavioral & Applied Management, 13*(1), 5–23. Retrieved from http://www.ibam.com/pubs/jbam/articles/vol13/Article_1_Blaskovich.pdf

Boisot, M., & McKelvey, B. (2010). Integrating modernist and postmodernist perspectives on organizations: A complexity science bridge. *Academy of Management Review, 35*(3), 415–433. doi:10.5465/AMR.2010.51142028

Brinkmann, J. (2013). Combining risk and responsibility perspectives: First steps. *Journal of Business Ethics, 112*(4), 567–583. doi:10.1007/s10551-012-1558-1

Brock, M. E., Vert, A., Kligyte, V., Waples, E. P., Sevier, S. T., & Mumford, M. D. (2008). Mental models: An alternative evaluation of a sensemaking approach to ethics instruction. *Science & Engineering Ethics, 14*(3), 449–472. doi:10.1007/s11948-008-9076-3

Brunswicker, S., & Hutschek, U. (2010). Crossing horizons: Leveraging cross-industry innovation search in the front-end of the innovation process. *International Journal of Innovation Management, 14*(4), 683–702. doi:10.1142/S1363919610002829

Burnes, B. (2004). Kurt Lewin and the planned approach to change: A re-appraisal. *Journal of Management Studies, 41*(6), 977–1002. doi:10.1111/j.14676486.2004 .00463.x

Cinite, I., Duxbury, L. E., & Higgins, C. (2009). Measurement of perceived organizational readiness for change in the public sector. *British Journal of Management, 20*(2), 265–277. doi:10.1111/j.1467-8551.2008.00582.x

Clyde-Smith, J. (2014). Utilising enterprise risk management strategies to develop a governance and operations framework for a new research complex: A case study. *Journal of Higher Education Policy & Management, 36*(3), 327–337. doi:10.1080/01587919.2014.899051

Colquitt, L. L., Hoyt, R. E., & Lee, R. B. (1999). Integrated risk management and the role of the risk manager. *Risk Management & Insurance Review, 2*(3), 43-61. doi:10.1111/j.1540-6296.1999.tb00003.x

The Committee of Sponsoring Organizations. (2004). *Enterprise risk management: Integrated framework.* New York, NY: Author.

Cooper, T., Faseruk, A., & Khan, S. (2013). Examining practitioner studies to explore ERM and organizational culture. *Journal of Management Policy & Practice, 14*(1), 53–68. Retrieved from http://www.na-businesspress.com/JMPP/CooperT_Web14_1_.pdf

Daud, W. N. W., Haron, H., & Ibrahim, D. N. (2011). The role of quality board of directors in enterprise risk management practices: Evidence from binary logistic regression. *International Journal of Business & Management, 6*(12), 205–211. doi:10.5539/ijbm.v6n12p205

De Jong, J. P. (2013). The decision to exploit opportunities for innovation: A study of high-tech small-business owners. *Entrepreneurship: Theory & Practice, 37*(2), 281–301. doi:10.1111/j.1540-6520.2011.00459.x

Di Serio, L. C. D., de Oliveira, L. H., & Schuch, L. M. S. (2011). Organizational risk management: A case study in companies that have won the Brazilian quality award prize. *Journal of Technology Management & Innovation, 6*(2), 230–243. Retrieved from http://www.scielo.cl/scielo.php/script_sci_serial/pid_0718-2724/lng_es/nrm_iso

Douglas M. (1978). *Cultural bias.* London, England: Royal Anthropological Institute.

Eckles, D. L., Hoyt, R. E., & Miller, S. M. (2014). The impact of enterprise risk management on the marginal cost of reducing risk: Evidence from the insurance industry. *Journal of Banking & Finance, 43*, 247–261. doi:10.1016/j.jbankfin.2014.02.007

Farrell, M., & Gallagher, R. (2015). The valuation implications of enterprise risk management maturity. *Journal of Risk & Insurance, 82*(3), 625–657. doi:10.1111/jori.12035

Fraser, J. S., Schoening-Thiessen, K., & Simkins, B. J. (2008). Who reads what most often? A survey of enterprise risk management literature read by risk executives. *Journal of Applied Finance, 18*(1), 73–91. doi:10.1002/9781118267080.ch22

Gates, S. (2006). Incorporating strategic risk into enterprise risk management: A survey of current corporate practice. *Journal of Applied Corporate Finance, 18*(4), 81–90. doi:10.1111/j.1745-6622.2006.00114.x

Gates, S., Nicolas, J., & Walker, P. L. (2012). Enterprise risk management: A process for enhanced management and improved performance. *Management Accounting Quarterly, 13*(3), 28-38. Retrieved from http://EconPapers.repec.org/RePEc:hal:journl:hal-0085 7435

Gioia, D. A., & Chittipeddi, K. (1991). Sensemaking and sensegiving in strategic change initiation. *Strategic Management Journal, 12*(6), 433-448. doi:10.1002/smj.4250120604

Gioia, D. A., & Thomas, J. B. (1996). Identity, image, and issue interpretation: Sensemaking during strategic change in academia. *Administrative Science Quarterly, 41*(3), 370-403. doi:10.2307/2393936

Gioia, D. A., Thomas, J. B., Clark, S. M., & Chittipeddi, K. (1994). Symbolism and strategic change in academia: The dynamics of sensemaking and influence. *Organization Science, 5*(3), 363-383. doi:10.1287/orsc.5.3.363

Gordon, L. A., Loeb, M. P., & Tseng, C. (2009). Enterprise risk management and firm performance: A contingency perspective. *Journal of Accounting & Public Policy, 28*(4), 301-327. doi:10.1016/j.jaccpubpol.2009.06.006

Grabowski, M., & Roberts, K. (1997). Risk mitigation in large-scale systems: Lessons from high reliability organizations. *California Management Review, 39*(4), 152-162. doi:10.2307/41165914

Grace, M. F., Leverty, J. T., Phillips, R. D., & Shimpi, P. (2015). The value of investing in enterprise risk management. *Journal of Risk & Insurance, 82*(2), 289. doi:10.1111/jori.12022

Gupta, P. K. (2011). Risk management in Indian companies: EWRM concerns and issues. *Journal of Risk Finance, 12*(2), 121. doi:10.1108/15265941111112848

Hallowell, M. R., Molenaar, K. R., & Fortunato, B. R. (2013). Enterprise risk management strategies for state departments of transportation. *Journal of Management in Engineering, 29*(2), 114-121. doi:10.1061/(ASCE)ME.1943-5479.0000136

Hayne, C., & Free, C. (2014). Hybridized professional groups and institutional work: COSO and the rise of enterprise risk management. *Accounting, Organizations, & Society, 39*, 309-330. doi:10.1016/j.aos.2014.05.002

Higgins, M. C., Weiner, J., & Young, L. (2012). Implementation teams: A new lever for organizational change. *Journal of Organizational Behavior, 33*(3), 366-388. doi:10.1002/job.1773

Holter, I., & Schwartz-Barcott, D. (1993). Action research: What is it? How has it been used and how can it be used in nursing? *Journal of Advanced Nursing, 18*(2), 298-304. doi:10.1046/j.1365-2648.1993.18020298.x

Hoyt, R. E., & Liebenberg, A. P. (2011). The value of enterprise risk management. *Journal of Risk & Insurance, 78*(4), 795. doi:10.2307/41350401

Hsu, S. H., Wang, Y. C., & Tzeng, S. F. (2007). The source of innovation: Boundary spanner. *Total Quality Management & Business Excellence, 18*(10), 1133-1145. doi:10.1080/14783360 701596274

Huber, M., & Rothstein, H. (2013). The risk organisation: Or how organisations reconcile themselves to failure. *Journal of Risk Research, 16*(6), 651-675. doi:10.1080/13669877 .2012.761276

Iyer, S. R., Rogers, D. A., & Simkins, B. J. (2010). Academic research on enterprise risk management. In J. Fraser & B. J. Simkins (Eds.), *Enterprise risk management* (pp. 419-439). Hoboken, NJ: John Wiley & Sons.

Jiang, N., & Carpenter, V. (2013). A case study of issues of strategy implementation in internationalization of higher education. *International Journal of Educational Management, 27*(1), 4-18. doi:10.1108/09513541311289792

Jongbloed, B., Enders, J., & Salerno, C. (2008). Higher education and its communities: Interconnections, interdependencies, and a research agenda. *Higher Education, 56*(3), 303-324. doi:10.1007/s10734-   008-9128-2

Kallenberg, K. (2009). Operational risk management in Swedish industry: Emergence of a new risk paradigm? *Risk Management, 11*(2), 90. doi:10.1057/rm.2009.6

Kanhai, C., Ganesh, L., & Muhwandavaka, R. (2014). An investigation of the extent of adoption of enterprise risk management by banks in Zimbabwe. *International Journal of Business & Commerce,* 3(7), 19. Retrieved from http://www.ijbcnet.com/3-7/IJBC-14-3703.pdf

Kaplan, R. S., & Mikes, A. (2012). Managing risks: A new framework. *Harvard Business Review, 90*(6), 48-60. Retrieved from https://hbr.org/2012/06/managing-risks-a-new   - framework

Kezar, A. J. (2014). *How colleges change: Understanding, leading, and enacting change.* New York, NY: Routledge.

Kezar, A., & Eckel, P. (2002). The effect of institutional culture on change strategies in higher education: Universal principles or culturally responsive concepts? *The Journal of Higher Education, 4*, 435. doi:10.1353/jhe.2002.0038

Kim, D. H., & Senge, P. M. (1994). Putting systems thinking into practice. *System Dynamics Review, 10*(2/3), 277-290. doi:10.1002/sdr.4260100213

Kimbrough, R. L., & Componation, P. J. (2009). The relationship between organizational culture and enterprise risk management. *Engineering Management Journal, 21*(2), 18-26. doi:10.1080/10429247.2009.11431803

Kleffner, A. E., Lee, R. B., & McGannon, B. (2003). The effect of corporate governance on the use of enterprise risk management: Evidence from Canada. *Risk Management & Insurance Review, 6*(1), 53-73. doi:10.1111/1098-1616.00020

Landsittel, D., & Rittenberg, L. (2010). COSO: Working with the academic community. *Accounting Horizons, 24*(3), 455-469. doi:10.2308/acch.2010.24.3.455

Leseure, M. J., Bauer, J., Birdi, K., Neely, A., & Denyer, D. (2004). Adoption of promising practices: A systematic review of the evidence. *International Journal of Management Reviews, 5/6*(3/4), 169-190. doi:10.1111/j.1460-8545.2004.00102

Liebenberg, A. P., & Hoyt, R. E. (2003). The determinants of enterprise risk management: Evidence from the appointment of chief risk officers. *Risk Management & Insurance Review, 6*(1), 37-52. doi:10.1111/1098-1616.00019

Lin, Y., Wen, M., & Yu, J. (2012). Enterprise risk management: Strategic antecedents, risk integration, and performance. *North American Actuarial Journal, 16*(1), 1-28. doi:10.1080/10920277.2012.10590630

Liu, J. Y., Zou, P., & Gong, W. (2013). Managing project risk at the enterprise level: Exploratory case studies in China. *Journal of Construction Engineering & Management, 139*(9), 1268-1274. doi:10.1061/(ASCE)CO.1943-7862.0000717

Louisot, P., & Ketcham, C. (Eds.). (2009). *Enterprise-wide risk management: Developing and implementing* (1st ed.). Malvern, PA: The Institutes.

Lundqvist, S. A. (2014). An exploratory study of enterprise risk management: Pillars of ERM. *Journal of Accounting, Auditing, & Finance, 29*(3), 393-429. doi:10.1177/0148558X145 35780

Lundqvist, S. A. (2015). Why firms implement risk governance: Stepping beyond traditional risk management to enterprise risk management. *Journal of Accounting & Public Policy. 34*(5), 441-446. doi:10.1016/j.jaccpubpol.2015.05.002

Maitlis, S. (2005). The social process of organizational sensemaking. *Academy of Management Journal, 48*(1), 21-49. doi:10.5465/AMJ.2005.15993111

March, J. G. (1994). *A primer on decision making: How decisions happen.* New York, NY: The Free Press.

March, J. G., & Shapira, Z. (1987). Managerial perspectives on risk and risk taking. *Management Science, 33*(11), 1404-1418. doi:10.1287/mnsc.33.11.1404

Mathrani, S., & Mathrani, A. (2013). Utilizing enterprise systems for managing enterprise risks. *Computers in Industry, 64*, 476-483. doi:10.1016/j.compind.2013.02.002

McCasky, M. B. (1982). *The executive challenge: Managing change and ambiguity.* Marshfield, MA: Pitman.

McKenna, S. D. (1999). Maps of complexity and organizational learning. *Journal of Management Development, 18*(9), 772. doi:10.1108/02621719910300829

McShane, M. K., Nair, A., & Rustambekov, E. (2011). Does enterprise risk management increase firm value? *Journal of Accounting, Auditing, & Finance, 26*(4), 641. doi:10.1177/0148558X11409160

Mikes, A. (2008). Chief risk officers at crunch time: Compliance champions or business partners? *Journal of Risk Management in Financial Institutions, 2*(1), 7-25. doi:10.2139/ssrn.1138615

Mikes, A. (2009). Risk management and calculative cultures. *Management Accounting Research, 20*(1), 18-40. doi:10.1016/j.mar.2008.10.005

Mintzberg, H., & Westley, F. (1992). Cycles of organizational change. *Strategic Management Journal, 13*(92), 1339-1359. doi:10.1002/smj.4250130905

Mumford, M. D., Connelly, S., & Brown, R. P. (2008). Ethics training for scientists: Preliminary evidence of training effectiveness. *Ethics & Behavior, 18*(4), 315-339. doi:10.1080/10508420802487815

Muralidhar, K. (2010). Enterprise risk management in the Middle East oil industry: An empirical investigation across GCC countries. *International Journal of Energy Sector Management, 4*(1), 59. doi:10.1108/17506221011033107

North Carolina State University & Protiviti. (2015). Executive perspectives on top risk for 2015: Key issues being discussed in the boardroom and C-suite. Retrieved from http://www.protiviti.com/en-US/Documents/Surveys/NC-State-Protiviti-Survey-Top-Risks-2015.pdf

Onder, S., & Ergin, H. (2012). Determiners of enterprise risk management applications in Turkey: An empirical study with logistic regression model on the companies included in Istanbul stock exchange. *Business & Economic Horizons, 7*(1), 19–26. Retrieved from http://EconPapers.repec.org/RePEc:pdc:jrnbeh:v:7:y:2012:i:1:p:19-26

Orlikowski, W. J., & Hofman, J. D. (1997). An improvisational model for change management: The case of groupware technologies. *Sloan Management Review, 38*(2), 11–21. Retrieved from http://ccs.mit.edu/papers/CCSWP191/CCSWP191.html

Paape, L., & Speklé, R. F. (2012). The adoption and design of enterprise risk management practices: An empirical study. *European Accounting Review, 21*(3), 533–564. doi:10.2139/ssrn.1658200

Pagach, D., & Warr, R. (2011). The characteristics of firms that hire chief risk officers. *Journal of Risk & Insurance, 78*(1), 185–211. doi:10.1111/j.1539-6975.2010.01378.x

Palazzo, G., Krings, F., & Hoffrage, U. (2012). Ethical blindness. *Journal of Business Ethics, 109*(3), 323–338. doi:10.1007/s10551-011-1130-4

Popper, M., & Lipshitz, R. (2000). Organizational learning: Mechanisms, culture, and feasibility. *Management Learning, 31*(2), 181–196. doi:10.1177/1350507600312003

Power, M. (2007). *Organized uncertainty: Designing a world of risk management.* New York, NY: Oxford University Press.

Ravasi, D., & Schultz, M. (2006). Responding to organizational identity threats: Exploring the role of organizational culture. *Academy of Management Journal, 49*(3), 433-458. doi:10.5465/AMJ.2006.21794663

Riquelme, H. E. (2013). In search of entrepreneurial opportunities—an integrated model. *Journal of Enterprising Culture, 21*(3), 249-274. doi:10.1142/S0218495813500118

Roberts, K. H., & Bea, R. (2001). Must accidents happen? Lessons from high-reliability organizations. *Academy of Management Executive, 15*(3), 70-78. doi:10.5465/AME.2001 .5229613

Schein, E. H. (1993). On dialogue, culture, and organizational learning. *Organizational Dynamics, 22*(2), 40-51. doi:10.1016/0090-2616(93)90052-3

Schein, H. E. (2010). *Organizational culture and leadership.* San Francisco, CA: John Wiley & Sons.

Scott, W. R. (1992). *Organizations: Rational, natural, and open systems* (3rd ed.). Englewood Cliffs, NJ: Prentice-Hall.

Scott, R. W. (2014). *Institutions and organizations: Ideas, interests, and identities.* Thousand Oaks, CA: Sage.

Senge, P. M. (1990). *The fifth discipline.* New York, NY: Doubleday.

Silva, E. S., Wu, Y., & Ojiako, U. (2013). Developing risk management as a competitive capability. *Strategic Change, 22*(5), 281. doi:10.1002/jsc.1940

Simkins, B. (2008). Enterprise risk management: Current initiatives and issues journal of applied finance roundtable. *Journal of Applied Finance, 18*(1), 115-132. Retrieved from http://www.fma.org

Smerek, R. E. (2013). Sensemaking and new college presidents: A conceptual study of the transition process. *Review of Higher Education, 36*(3), 371-403. doi:10.1353/rhe.2013.0028

Sonenshein, S. (2007). The role of construction, intuition, and justification in responding to ethical issues at work: The sensemaking-intuition model. *Academy of Management Review, 32*(4), 1022-1040. doi:10.5465/AMR.2007.26585677

Stewart, A. C., Williams, J., Smith-Gratto, K., Black, S. S., & Kane, B. T. (2011). Examining the impact of pedagogy on student application of learning: Acquiring, sharing, and using knowledge for organizational decision making. *Decision Sciences Journal of Innovative Education, 9*(1), 3-26. doi:10.1111/j.1540-4609.2010.00288.x

Stigliani, I., & Ravasi, D. (2012). Organizing thoughts and connecting brains: Material practices and the transition from individual to group-level prospective sensemaking. *Academy of Management Journal, 55*(5), 1232-1259. doi:10.5465/amj.2010.0890

Suchman, M. C. (1995). Managing legitimacy: Strategic and institutional approaches. *Academy of Management Review, 20*(3), 571-610. doi:10.5465/AMR.1995.9508080331

Sun, P. T., & Anderson, M. H. (2010). An examination of the relationship between absorptive capacity and organizational learning, and a proposed integration. *International Journal of Management Reviews, 12*(2), 130-150. doi:10.1111/j.1468-2370.2008.00256.x

Tekathen, M., & Dechow, N. (2013). Enterprise risk management and continuous re-alignment in the pursuit of accountability: A German case. *Management Accounting Research, 24*, 100-121. doi:10.1016/j.mar.2013.04.005

Thomas, J. B., Sussman, S., & Henderson, J. C. (2001). Understanding "strategic learning": Linking organizational learning, knowledge management, and sensemaking. *Organization Science, 12*(3), 331-345. Retrieved from http://pubsonline.informs.org /journal/orsc

Thomas, T., & Lamm, E. (2012). Legitimacy and organizational sustainability. *Journal of Business Ethics, 110*(2), 191-203. doi:10.1007/s10551-012-1421-4

University Risk Management and Insurance Association. (2007). *URMIA white paper: ERM in higher education.* Retrieved from http://www.urmia.org/library/docs/reports/URMIA _ERM_White_Paper.pdf

Van de Ven, A. H., & Poole, M. (1995). Explaining development and change in organizations. *Academy of Management Review, 20*(3), 510-540. doi:10.5465/AMR.1995.9508080329

Wall, E. (2011). Structure of meaning and sense-making of risk: An operationalisation of sense-making tested by grouping individuals according to their structure of meaning. *Journal of Risk Research, 14*(6), 735-755. doi:10.1080/13669877.2011.571772

Weick, K. E. (1995). *Sensemaking in organizations.* Thousand Oaks, CA: Sage.

Weick, K. E. (2007). The experience of theorizing. In K. G. Smith & M. A. Hitt (Eds.), *Great minds in management* (pp. 355-372). New York, NY: Oxford University Press.

Weick, K. E., & Sutcliffe, K. M. (2006). Mindfulness and the quality of organizational attention. *Organization Science, 17*(4), 514-524. Retrieved from http://pubsonline.informs.org /journal/orsc

Weick, K. E., & Sutcliffe, K. M. (2007). *Managing the unexpected: Resilient performance in an age of uncertainty* (2nd ed.). San Francisco, CA: Jossey-Bass, Publishers, Inc.

Weick, K. E., Sutcliffe, K. M., & Obstfeld, D. (2005). Organizing and the process of sensemaking. *Organization Science, 4,* 409. doi:10.2307/25145979

Wicks, D. (2001). Institutionalized mindsets of invulnerability: Differentiated institutional fields and the antecedents of organizational crisis. *Organization Studies, 22*(4), 659-692. doi:10.1177/0170840601224005

Williams, S., Zainuba, M., & Jackson, R. (2008). Determinants of managerial risk perceptions and intentions. *Journal of Management Research, 8*(2), 59-75. Retrieved from http://jmr.indianjournals.com/jmr.aspx?target=ijor:jmr&vol ume=1&issue=4&article =editorial

Wood, M. D., Bostrom, A., Bridges, T., & Linkov, I. (2012). Cognitive mapping tools: Review and risk management needs. *Risk Analysis, 32*(8), 1333-1348. doi:10.1111/j.15396924.2011.01767.x

Wood, R., & Bandura, A. (1989). Social cognitive theory of organizational management. *Academy of Management Review, 14*(3), 361-384. doi:10.5465/AMR.1989.4279067

Woon, F. L., Azizan, N. A., & Samad, F. F. (2011). A strategic framework for value enhancing enterprise risk management. *Journal of Global Business & Economics, 2*(1), 23-47. Retrieved from http://EconPapers.repec.org/RePEc:grg:01biss:v:2:y:2011:i:1: p:23-47

Zhao, X., Hwang, B., & Low, S. P. (2013). Critical success factors for enterprise risk management in Chinese construction companies. *Construction Management & Economics, 31*(12), 1199-1214. doi:10.1080/01446193.2013.867521

Zhao, X., Hwang, B., & Low, S. P. (2014a). Enterprise risk management implementation in construction firms: An organizational change perspective. *Management Decision, 52*(5), 814-833. doi:10.1108/MD-02-2014-0082

Zhao, X., Hwang, B., & Low, S. P. (2014b). Investigating enterprise risk management maturity in construction firms. *Journal of Construction Engineering & Management, 140*(8), 1. doi:10.1061/(ASCE)CO.1943-7862.0000873

Zhao, X., Hwang, B., & Low, S. P. (2015). Enterprise risk management in international construction firms: Drivers and hindrances. *Engineering Construction & Architectural Management, 22*(3), 347-366. doi:10.1108/ECAM-09-2014-0117